HIS MOSAIC MASTERPIECE

HIS MOSAIC MASTERPIECE

ELIZABETH TROYLYNN

Fitting Words

His Mosaic Masterpiece

Published in conjunction with Fitting Words LLC

www.fittingwords.net

ISBN-13: 978-1-7379244-1-8 (hardcover)
ISBN: 978-1-7379244-6-3 (softcover)

1 2 3 4 5—26 25 24 23 22
Printed in the United States of America

Fitting Words

Acknowledgements

I want to thank God most of all, because without God I wouldn't be able to do any of this.

To my daughters, Alyssa and Troylynn

You both are the greatest accomplishments and the greatest successes I have ever achieved.
I love you both so much.
So proud of you. Always be you.
What a blessing it is to be your mom.

To my grandchildren, Josiah and Alana

I will always treasure our time together.
I cherish each of you!
What a blessing it is to be your mum-mum.
You are the most perfect you of yourself.
I love you both so much and am very proud of you both.

To my best friend, Corky

My sister in heart. I always wanted a sister and so blessed it was you. Thank you for always loving me for me.
I will always cherish our sister talks.
Love you! Follow your dreams!

To my brothers

I love you brothers more than you could even imagine.
I am so grateful for my brothers. I will never forget the important role that each of you have played in my life.
I will always be there for each of you.

To my foster parents

Without you both I would not be where I am today. All of your sacrifices and your hard work will never be forgotten. I am in awe of you. I have so much respect for you. Thank you for everything you did for me. I love you both!

To my adopted parents who are in heaven

One of the greatest memories I will always have from you is introducing me to the gifts of nature. The camping trips to the Colorado mountains is something that I will never forget. Nature has taught me how to be truly present and have awareness in my daily life.

My sincere appreciation, gratitude and Thank you to everyone on my publishing team. I have met some amazing, talented people over the years. I had a dream to help others. Each one of you played a big part of putting the pieces together. This has been an amazing journey. I have learned so much from each of you that will never be forgotten.

I want to thank EVERYONE who I have meet on this amazing journey we call life. For those who have supported me personally and professionally. Know that your positive words have helped me to better myself each day. I am so grateful for each of you.

All of your support will never be forgotten.

Contents

You cannot question every season of your
life when you do not understand
the purpose of it because God's provisions are often hidden.
God has plans that we cannot understand
until we get there... and you'll say, now I understand
why I had to go through it!
Now I understand why it had to hurt!
Now I understand why that pain had to afflict me,
because God knew there was going to be someone
else who would have that pain.
Now I can share!
I'm not happy that it happened,
but I guess I had to be there...
I guess I was part of your purpose, God.

—Pastor Steven Furtick

Broken pieces take time to fit together to become a mosaic masterpiece of a beautiful you to impact the world.

PROLOGUE

Setting the Stage

In this story of my life, some of the chapters begin with a description of contemporary events, intended to give the reader context for what was happening in the larger world. Decisions that made sense fifty years ago might seem wrongheaded today. All I can say is this: they made sense at the time.

My story begins in Colorado in the 1960s. Colorado is still one of my favorite places to be, and I get to take the most beautiful photos of the mountains. But the 1960s were a radical time when great change spread across the country. Those changes spread at different speeds across the nation, and, depending on where you lived, change could take a while to reach you. The coasts were affected first. Where I was, in Northglenn, Colorado, change came more slowly. Not every young person was a hippie, protesting the war, taking drugs, and engaging in what they called "free love." In fact, many hippies were from upper-class families—it took *money* to live without working. Even if I wanted to, I could never have afforded to be a hippie! And I was only five years old in 1966 anyway.

Ever since the end of World War II, the United States had been the most powerful country in the world. We were afraid of nuclear war with the USSR, but by and large most Americans lived comfortable lives. The income of a single person was enough to live on, so for married couples, the husband usually worked while his wife stayed home. Plenty of factory jobs were available, so most people did not need a college education to earn a living.

However, life in the 1950s and early 1960s was a lot less comfortable if you weren't white, and the fight for civil rights occupied much of the news. In parts of the country—mostly in the South—racism remained legalized. Public facilities could be labeled "For Whites Only," and an inferior, less-convenient facility would be designated "Colored Only." Although the term "colored" was even then falling out of favor, housing, schools, restaurants—even restrooms and water fountains—were still restricted to one race or another. Prejudice also existed against other races, but you rarely heard about civil rights protests by Hispanics, Asians, or Native Americans (who were just called "Indians" back then). The LGBTQ+ community wasn't even discussed, except as the punch line to a joke. The Stonewall riots were three years away.

In today's world of 2022, I am glad to see people working together to bring diversity into the workforce. Diversity in the world is important for many reasons, but primarily because we all have skills and opinions, and embracing those creates an environment that fosters respect for all, regardless of our differences, and cultural diversity brings out compassion instead of judgment. Everyone is unique and there is only one of you in this world. Be you! We all have a backstory.

Although white women were privileged in comparison to minorities in the '50s and '60s, even they did not have the same rights as men. Laws varied from state to state, but only after 1974 could a married woman get a bank loan unless it was cosigned by a male (usually her husband or father). This is when the Equal Credit Act was passed.

When my story began, the president was Lyndon Baines Johnson, a Democrat from Texas. He had been vice president but became president when John Fitzgerald Kennedy was assassinated in 1963. (I was barely a toddler; too young to remember that.) Johnson did several good things with his War on Poverty and his Civil Rights programs, but his support of the Vietnam War overshadowed all of that. Johnson kept sending more troops to Southeast Asia, and many young men refused to go. There were massive protests against the war.

A lot of people who lived through 1966 remember it fondly; they forget how nervous people were. People feared nuclear war, “disrespectful” youth, anti-war protests, and race riots.

But I was five years old, and I didn’t know about most of that. I just wanted to feel safe and loved and live with two caring parents. Unfortunately, that was not to be.

Chapter One

The Worst Night of My Life

"I found the kids!"

An unfamiliar male voice woke me from a sound sleep. I couldn't see who was speaking; he was aiming a flashlight at my face. I pulled my threadbare blanket tighter around me. The cheap fabric felt rough, but I didn't want a strange man to see me in my pajamas. Below me, on the bottom level of the bunk bed, I heard my youngest brother stirring. My bedroom was across the hall, but I liked sleeping above my brothers on the top bunk. Usually, I felt safe sleeping above them. Not tonight.

Another man entered the room and switched on the overhead light. Now I could see that they were policemen. The first man turned off his flashlight.

Backlit by the sole light in the room, their blue uniforms looked black and sinister. Frightened, I pulled the blanket over my head.

The second policeman approached and bent down to talk to my little brother. "Everything's OK, son," he said. "But I need you to get up and get dressed." He stood and addressed me. "You, too, darling—get up." He was a smoker. I could smell the tobacco on his breath, even with the thin blanket covering my head.

Instead of doing what he asked, I curled up, pulling the blanket tighter around me.

The policeman reached out, pulled my blanket away, and effortlessly picked me up. I was embarrassed that a stranger would see me in my pajamas. He gently set me down on the floor. It was cold on my bare feet. Nights in Colorado are often cold.

I have two brothers, but my older brother was missing, and my younger brother was whimpering with fear. Or perhaps that was me. I was certainly terrified.

Where was my mother? My father didn't live there. My parents had divorced three years before, and my mother had full custody of us.

I looked around. My youngest brother found the clothes he'd worn that day and put them on. Hurried along by one of the policemen, I went to my room to get dressed. Like most boys, my brothers didn't care if they wore dirty clothes, but I wanted to wear clean clothes. However, my sole dresser was empty. Reluctantly, I dressed in the clothes I'd changed out of several hours before. They were the only clothes in my hamper.

I assumed my mother was in the living room. This wasn't the first time the police had come to our home, but usually they were called to stop a fight between my mother and one of her boyfriends. But when I emerged from my bedroom and walked down the hall, my mother was nowhere in sight. Instead, my older brother was in the kitchen, stuffing clothes—children's clothes—into three paper bags. That was why my bureau was empty; he had stuffed all my clothes into one of those bags. We didn't have much in the way of possessions. Just about everything I owned fit into a single paper grocery bag.

Eventually, my oldest brother explained what had happened. Something had awakened him during the night. He had gone into the living room to find our mother unconscious on the kitchen floor. Medical? Alcohol? Drugs? A suicide attempt? Had my mother possibly called the police prior to losing consciousness? I had so many questions, but answers weren't coming. How did the police know to take my brothers and me to our Aunt Rachel's house? Perhaps the police knew from the previous times they'd been called to break up fights between my mother and her boyfriend. We were too young to have known the address, but they took us right to Aunt Rachel's, Mom's sister.

Maybe my brother had walked next door to get help—the houses were close together in our neighborhood of

Northglenn. Perhaps he had gotten the neighbor to call for an ambulance or someone called from my house. I still remember to this day every part of our house. The phone was in our kitchen, bright yellow, and it hung on the wall.

Fifty years later, we can't remember how the police were summoned, but the rest of that night is a memory I will never forget.

Through the open front door, I saw my mother on a gurney, being loaded into an ambulance. Some adult—a policeman or an EMT, I was not sure—said they'd take her to the hospital at Fort Logan. This hospital helps those who are dealing with something mentally. After the ambulance left, the policemen guided us outside toward their cruiser. On the sidewalk, one of them spotted something. It was one of my mother's shoes. I ran over and picked it up. Crying openly, I held the shoe tightly and refused to let it go. The police officers let me have it. My brothers and I got into the back of the police cruiser, and one of the men put our three paper grocery bags of clothes in the trunk. Then both policemen got in the front and drove us away. Little did my brothers and I know that this was the last time we'd ever be in our home. We never got to go back.

It was late winter of 1967, and I was five years old. My life would never be the same. In a six months, America would enter what was called "The Summer of Love," but it would not seem that way to me.

Chapter Two

My Father

My father was named Lawrence Charles Lindberg; "Lucky Lindy" was his nickname, just like the famous aviator. He was born on September 5, 1934, in Minneapolis, Minnesota. Of course 1934 was the height of the Great Depression, and his family suffered terribly. Although we've had recessions in recent years, we have experienced nothing as severe as the Great Depression. In 1931, Minneapolis saw food riots by hungry people. The social welfare net we enjoy these days simply didn't exist back then. Thousands of banks failed, leaving their depositors penniless. As a result, President Franklin Delano Roosevelt created the Federal Deposit Insurance Corporation (FDIC) in 1933, which insured bank deposits. The next year, the Securities and Exchange Commission was formed to oversee the stock market.

Social Security was created in August 1935. Before that, if you became too ill or old to work, you either depended on relatives or starved. I am sure there are probably still many people for whom this is the case. As a nation, we are not great at taking care of our most vulnerable. But Social Security was a start.

In the Great Depression, people often had just enough money to buy a cup of tea. No food, mind you. Just a cup of hot water and a single tea bag, purchased at a lunch counter. But, as soon as the restaurant staff wasn't looking, the hungry person would grab the bottle of ketchup off the counter and pour it into their cup of hot water. Then they'd have a makeshift bowl of tomato soup. It wasn't much, but it was enough for a starving person to survive another day. What a dismal way to live!

Almost one in four people were unemployed during the Great Depression, which lasted almost ten years. It was a dark time in the country's history, and many people suffered terribly. And if you were going to be broke—and perhaps homeless—Minneapolis wasn't a good place to be. Minneapolis is one of the coldest cities in the country, and without food and shelter, it could get dangerous quickly.

Over the years I discovered I have a lot of family living in Minneapolis, including my father's family. One of his siblings explained that their mother, my grandmother, struggled with hard times during the Depression, to the point that she had to put her children into temporary foster care. My birth father made the choice to not go into foster care. Instead, he joined the US Air Force, and he served during the Korean conflict.

During World War II, the US Air Force had been part of the US Army. It only became a separate branch of the military in September 1947, under President Harry Truman. Women were admitted to the Air Force in 1948, the same year that Truman issued an executive order that began the racial integration of all branches of the military. The Korean War was the first major military conflict after World War II.

The Korean conflict lasted from 1950 to 1953. The US Air Force was heavily involved because North Korea was extensively bombed. This was the first war in which jet fighters faced each other in air-to-air combat. (North Korea's fighters were provided by their Soviet allies.) The US never formally declared war on North Korea; President Truman referred to it as a "police action." Whatever it was called, it was a terribly destructive conflict. Some three million Koreans died—proportionately, more people than were killed in any one country during World War II.

We don't know where in Korea my father served. All we know for sure is that after the war, he was never the same again. Unfortunately, this was a common story for so many. I wish I'd known him before he went off to war. I really wish I had experienced the father-daughter memories that we should have had but didn't. When I do see healthy father-daughter relationships, it reminds me of what my father and I never had and the many reasons why.

We all only have one life on this earth, and my life and that of my father didn't work out the way I'd hoped. I'm not sure if he made some bad choices or if this would have happened regardless. I wasn't born until after my father became a wounded veteran, damaged in mind and body. He was twenty-seven years old when I was born; I was his only daughter.

After my father moved to Colorado, I don't believe he had much face-to-face contact with his family in Minnesota. One of my birth aunts told me years later, when we connected briefly, that my birth mother met my father's relatives a few times. His three stepsisters came and visited them after my older brother was born. My aunt also told me that their stepbrother, my father, was very much in love with my mother. However, their impression of my mother was that she seemed rather cold. One of my aunts, who was only eighteen at the time, claimed that my mother said, "Stop telling your brother [my father] to get me pregnant!" As it happened, my mother was already pregnant with me at the time, and they had already had another child before me.

My father's family in Minnesota had plenty of hard times. My paternal grandfather, Lawrence Clifford Lindberg, was born in 1904. When he died in 1963, I was two years old. He served in the US Army during World War II from 1942 to 1943, and he passed away in

1963. My grandmother and grandfather at some point divorced, and he then remarried. Once she was single, my grandmother, Emma Jean Lindberg, could no longer support all her children; she had to put them into temporary foster care. My father, who was almost an adult at this point, decided to join the US Air Force rather than join the other children in foster care.

My paternal grandmother, Emma Jean, was born in March 1913 and died in September 1996. I was thirty-five years old when she died and had never met her. I wonder if she ever knew about my brothers and me.

My father was originally trained as a dental assistant in the Air Force. I have no idea how he switched from a behind-the-lines soldier to a combatant. The personnel files that might have explained that were destroyed in a fire on July 12, 1973, in a disastrous conflagration at the National Personnel Records Center (NPRC) in St. Louis, Missouri. That fire destroyed between sixteen and eighteen million official military personnel files, including the one belonging to my father.

My father was sent to fight in the Korean War. At some point he was captured by the North Koreans, who tortured him. My aunts still remember the awful notice they received from the military, explaining that their stepbrother had been captured.

Like many war veterans, my father did not readily talk about his experiences. However, he returned home with a physical injury that he could not hide; his left hand was damaged and some of his fingernails were missing. He had only partial use of his left hand. One of my father's stepsisters told me that the North Koreans had nailed his hands to a table! They drove the nails right through his fingernails, which is why some of them were missing. I cannot imagine what my father went through or how anyone moves on after something like that. It would change anyone forever.

After he was discharged from the Air Force, my father moved to Colorado and met my mother, Helen. They were married on January 9, 1960, in Berthoud, Colorado. My two brothers and I were born during their short marriage, which ended in divorce in 1964, just as the British Invasion began—a much different kind of conflict. British rock and roll bands became popular in the US. The Beatles, the Animals, the Dave Clark Five, Herman's Hermits, the Rolling Stones, and others took over the top spots on the American Hit Parade. It was a harbinger of things to come.

The term Post-Traumatic Stress Disorder (PTSD) had not been adopted in the 1960s, but my father displayed some of the symptoms. The term was first used in 1980, and it came to replace earlier terms such as "shell shock" and "combat fatigue." A search of criminal records in Colorado shows that my father was arrested multiple times after the divorce, for such violations as trespassing, property damage, carrying a concealed weapon, public intoxication, driving under the influence, and driving without a license or proof of insurance. He also couldn't hold down a job. My father had a lot of stress outbursts and angry moments. I think the trespassing charge was a result of him trying to see his children. If I lost my children, I would have tons of anxiety, worry, and may not make the best choices. What would you do if you lost your children?

My parents' divorce records claim spousal abuse, although there does not appear to be any record of an arrest for domestic violence. But the court papers claim "extreme and repeated acts of mental and physical cruelty." Those divorce proceedings were executed on May 19, 1964, in the County of Denver, Colorado. The divorce itself was granted on August 25, 1964. I was three years old.

One of my aunts later told me that my father was shattered by the divorce and hated having his children taken away from him. This is probably why he had legal issues shortly afterward. My father had no family in Colorado except his children. He never remarried. He never left Colorado to go back to Minneapolis where his family was.

I rarely saw my father after the divorce. He was granted visitation only once a week, on Sundays from 11:00 a.m. to 5:00 p.m. I still remember being with my dad on those days, remarkable given that I was so young. He used to take us to various restaurants, and we'd always sit in a booth with my brothers on each side of me and my father across from us. My legs would dangle when I sat—they were too short to reach the floor.

We were the children of a disabled veteran, so my brothers and I were entitled to what are called auxiliary child benefits. These payments went to my mother while we lived with her. Social Security records show that those benefits were paid—to me—from February 1964 through August 1978. Similar benefits were allocated for my brothers.

I never saw those auxiliary benefits. The Social Security office was not particularly cooperative. After my third visit, they finally disclosed to me who received the auxiliary benefits that continued after my adoption until I was eighteen. My adoptive father received all the checks that came from my birth father's Social Security. Prior to that, I was not aware that money was given to adoptive parents, although mine deserved that money to help with the family expenses. The benefits were the same amount of money, around sixty dollars, that my mother received monthly, but when we were adopted, the funds were transferred to my adoptive parents.

I lost touch with my father while I was living with my mother, but it wasn't my choice. Around 1998, I found my father through Social Security because my little brother, Victor, had his Social Security number. When Victor was born, he had some medical issues that developed into a leg disease called Legg-Calvé-Perthes. He had a lot of physical limitations that started as a child. He has had many challenges in his life. The records show that he was getting assistance through my father's Social Security, so I called the agency to ask how I could reach my father and was told I could write a letter and they would forward it to him. I prayed that my father would receive my letter!

A few weeks later, I received a collect call from my father. I thought it was very odd that he called me collect, but I wanted to connect with him, so I accepted the call. He said, "This is Larry."

I was in disbelief. He'd really called me! My heart was so full of emotion. After a few minutes of conversation, he asked, "Where is your mother? Where is Helen?" I told him I had no idea where she was. My father asked me again in a very worried tone, "What do you mean, you do not know where she is?"

I said, "You don't know?"

My father answered, "Know what?"

"My brothers and I went into foster care, then we were adopted," I told him. "I thought you knew." He became very upset and raised his voice. I still today remember how worried he sounded.

Then there were a few moments of silence. My father asked if his children were OK and wanted to know where we all lived, what family we went to, and what they were like. I told him what I could, but I wasn't able to share why we had to go into foster care, then adoption, since I did not have any court documents. I asked my father if he knew anything about the adoption and he said that he didn't. I asked him if he had any pictures of me or my brothers when we were younger that I could look at or have. I was not fortunate enough to see or have any baby pictures of me or my brothers. I have no idea what I looked like as a baby. That privilege was taken away from me and my brothers. My father said he had no pictures and that my mother had kept them.

I was living in Pennsylvania at the time. He said I could come to Denver and visit him but I would have to write him a letter to let him know when I was coming because he didn't have a phone. A week later, he sent me a Christmas card. I still have that card and will never let it go. He signed the card, "Larry." I think he didn't feel that he had a right to sign it "Dad" after all those years.

A few months went by, and I purchased a plane ticket to Denver and then wrote a letter to my father as he had directed me to do to let him know when I would arrive. I was excited but nervous. What would I say to him? Was he in good health, a stable mental state? What was his house like? Would I get a response?

In a few weeks, the letter came back to me with a notification from the post office that he did not live at that address anymore and there was no forwarding address. My heart sank. I sat on the floor and cried. My father had given me hope that at least one of my parents loved me, but that was not the case. It was such a terrible realization to face again! I was very sad for a long time. I kept praying to God that there was a good reason and one day I would know what it was. Was I being saved from something? I kept wondering, *What is wrong with me that my parents could not love me from birth?* Now my father had a second chance and he'd blown it! I had to pray for God to help me through the pain and give me strength to heal again. There was nothing else I could do.

I continued with my life, but this disappointment would always follow me. I kept telling myself over and over that this door was not to open for me at this time for good reason.

In July 2013, a call from my brother Victor filled in some of the pieces. I remember that month because it was a hot summer, and I was recovering from foot surgery. The day of my surgery, before being put under in the operating room, I had looked around to see what the room looked like and who was there. The oddest thing was that I saw a tall man with glasses and short silver hair standing by the medical devices. I assumed he worked there. What got my attention was that he didn't seem to fit there; he was much older. Our eyes met, then he looked at me and smiled. I felt a peace I cannot explain. After my surgery, while I was in recovery, I looked for the tall gentleman and described him to my nurse. She had no idea whom I was talking about. As I look back, I feel that this man could have been my father's spirit watching over me.

When my brother called, he told me that he'd received a letter from Social Security telling him that as the child of a veteran he was entitled to receive a death benefit. That's how I learned about my father's death. Hearing this news was a shock to me and it broke my heart.

I find it very odd that my brother received such a letter. How did the Social Security Administration connect my brother with my father after my brother had been adopted for so many years? I truly believe to this day someone up in heaven wanted that letter sent to notify me and my brothers about my father's death. I believe there was a purpose to us knowing.

At that point, I just wanted to find out where my father was buried so I could finally talk to him, although it would have to be at his grave. I had many questions I had carried with me over the years. Now, sadly, I would get no answers. I looked up his name on the internet and, sure enough, I found the obituary. His children were not mentioned as survivors—only his three stepsisters (who live in Florida). He was buried in Fort Snelling National Cemetery, in North Minneapolis, Minnesota.

I contacted the cemetery to see if I could get any contact details of any family members. I wanted to know where my father had been and what happened, to know everything I could about him. One of the employees mentioned that my father had a representative who could provide me with contact details. I called right away and spoke to my father's representative in Denver, a woman named Susan, a bank employee who worked with veterans. Susan asked me many questions to verify I was who I said I was. I understood that. People come out of the woodwork when loved ones pass away. My conversation with her felt surreal—like I was dreaming but did not want to wake up. Susan told me there was an estate, which would be given to my father's blood children. However, she would need to talk to me and my brothers until she was satisfied that we were, in fact, Larry's birth children. I told her the truth: we had been adopted by someone else, and I did not expect all of this when I had called. I had simply wanted to connect with family. She asked to put me on hold for a few minutes. She wanted to put me in touch with my birth cousin, Shelly. She came back on to say Shelly wanted to connect with me! Susan gave me Shelly's number and said to call her right away. I agreed. I did find this a bit strange. Could Shelly have been looking for me and my brothers before I even called Susan, my father's representative?

I called Shelly shortly after. She lived in Montana. She started asking me all kinds of questions like where my brothers and I had been and why we hadn't been in Larry's life. I explained to her that we'd been in foster care and then had been adopted. I didn't know where my mother was. Shelly kept calling me for the next two weeks asking me more and more questions. I told her the truth; I had nothing to hide. She, on the other hand, had a reason for all her questions that I didn't know about until much later.

As I waited for more information from Shelly, I continued to try searching for my father's records through the Veterans Administration. Their records showed that he died on May 11, 2013, at the Colorado State Veterans Home. But I discovered more talking to Shelly and Susan.

My father led a tragic life. The tragedy was compounded after my father hired a company to find his children. My father had given them our birth names; he did not know our adopted last names. The company that searched for my brothers and me could not locate us because our names had been changed at adoption.

As I discussed my father and his estate in more detail, the bank's attorney advised me to hire an attorney to stop the release of my father's estate to other family members. I could not believe that all of this was happening. All I had wanted was information about my father, but now it felt as if a fight was brewing between my father's representatives and my father's stepsiblings, as well as Shelly. It was going to be a difficult battle because of the adoption law in Colorado, but we had my father's representative, the bank's attorney, and the Veterans Affairs attorney wanting to fight for my father's wishes to be fulfilled. They knew he would have wanted all his possessions to go to his birth children. I thought that maybe, if we put up a fight, my father's stepsiblings would think about what my father had wanted.

Sadly, this did not happen. But if I had to challenge his estate again, I would absolutely do it. Neither my father's legal representative nor any of his family members ever helped him draw up a will. I reached out to my state representative to see why there was no law to help our veterans obtain a will to protect their wishes and was told that no one can be forced to make a will. But their representatives make money off their estates with administration fees. This seems wrong on so many levels. It infuriates me! My father died intestate, which means he had no will, and not one person whom he relied on helped him to make a will.

My father's wishes were never fulfilled. His representative, Susan, told me my father had severe Alzheimer's disease toward the end of his life. This is probably why he did not remember our conversation years ago when I found him. He did not know our new names or that we had been adopted. Susan also told me that my father was a very kind man. I have always felt that he was kind and wronged by the people whom he trusted in life to do the right thing by him.

One of my goals with this book is to share the story about what happened to my father and to speak on behalf of my father. If this can help even one of my readers, it'll have been worth it. That's the connection between parent and child that can't be taken away!

Please make every effort to make a will for yourself and your loved ones, to ensure that your wishes will be fulfilled. Please make a will and give a copy to an attorney and encourage your family members to do the same. Death can bring out pure hate and greed. When my father was dying, his representative at the bank did not work with my father to help him obtain a will. His representative told me that she was new to my father's case and his last caseworker should have encouraged him to protect his wishes but failed to do so. Susan said that she would have worked with him before his Alzheimer's disease got worse to make sure his last wishes were delivered upon his passing. But the fact remains that my father had searched for us. The search failed, so his wishes were not fulfilled. Why didn't his stepsiblings help him? His cousin, Shelly, whom I spoke to, mentioned that she would talk to my father on the phone, but she never met him. Why didn't she help him?

That is what sincere love is. Truth speaks for itself. If my father wanted his stepsiblings to receive his belongings, and if he really hated me and my brothers, then he would have made sure to have a will and put them on it. But he had no will, so the law says when someone passes on without a will, the estate goes to the next blood family member. In this case, that was my brothers and me.

Yet my father's estate did not go to my brothers and me because of the Colorado adoption law—it went to his stepsiblings. Because of what happened with my father's case, Susan told me that the bank opened all veterans' files to tell their clients about my father's story and try to encourage all veterans to complete their wills. At least a small act of goodness came from this because other veterans will obtain a will after hearing my father's story.

While I did connect much later with more of my birth family, not one of them made me feel like I was family. I felt like an outsider. My aunt Rachel, my mother's sister, did not want to meet or talk on the phone. Then I spoke to one of my father's stepsiblings, and they said it was my fault for not being in my father's life. Truly, they did not care what happened to me and my brothers!

Children don't choose to be adopted; adults make the choice for the child. I believe that when we all come to the end of our lives, we start to see a slideshow of how we treated people during our life. We will either have peace, or we'll fear what will happen to us after we pass. Some people will make peace with what they've done, and some will carry it with them. I also believe that when we do pass, it's not our family we will see first but the people we helped along the way in our one life.

My father's cousin, Shelly, was nice at first, but she was only trying to get all the info she could for the estate case. After she got what she needed, she said we could not talk anymore because there was going to be a fight for my father's estate. Shelly found my mother Helen and asked her to send a document declaring our adoption was legal. Why did she need to do this if I told the truth about the adoption? My birth mother and Shelly did a very hateful thing! What purpose did this serve? Karma always finds its way back to you when you hurt someone.

A coda to this story developed later. On October 18, 2019, I received a phone call around 7:00 p.m. I let the call go to voicemail. The woman's message said she was a cousin of Shelly, and she was trying to get in contact with the daughter of Larry Lindberg. She wanted to send me and my brothers a family history going back a hundred years to Norway. I didn't know how this person knew so much about me and my brothers. When I called her back that evening, I asked why she was calling and if she knew my cousin Shelly. Amazingly, after a few minutes of silence, she admitted it was her—Shelly.

What did she have to gain by pretending to be someone else? She admitted my brothers and I did nothing wrong in fighting for my father's last wishes to be fulfilled. She said my father loved us.

So why did she go against my father's last wishes if my father loved us so much? She told me one of my father's stepsiblings had recently died—one of the stepsiblings who received a part of my father's estate, the one who told me it was my fault that I was not in my father's life. Shelly also said the other stepsibling who had received part of my father's estate was not doing very well with her health.

This all confused me; I was not sure why Shelly wanted me to know this. Was Shelly trying to make herself look innocent?

Then, as we talked Shelly confessed that her life had been a tragedy since the case and she had gotten spiritual. Karma! Shelly also said she'd had a few dreams about my father, and he told her to give each one of his children one hundred dollars. I didn't believe her; my father never would have done that! The dreams Shelly described reminded me more of the movie *Ghost* with Patrick Swayze, Demi Moore, and Whoopi Goldberg!

But what they took from my father was so much more than money or possessions—they robbed him of his last wishes. I consider myself a pretty strong woman, but this was a moment in life that took me to the edge. A few days after my conversation with Shelly

I started having a very bad headache that ended up being a hemiplegic migraine. This is a rare and serious type of migraine, the symptoms of which mimic the signs of a stroke. I had to stay in the hospital overnight and had many tests done. Thank goodness I have not had another one!

My father's stepsisters and my cousin will never know how much pain they have caused through their unkind actions, and no amount of money can fix what they did. My father had a lot of sentimental items that we would have liked to have, such as the military flag from his funeral and the watch he always wore. Shelly has tried to assuage her shame and guilt by sending us a family history from Norway and a $100 bill. But she still has not done the right thing.

But I have had to forgive them and move past this. I will see my father one day in heaven. I do feel him at times by little signs he sends to me. I truly believe God is still taking care of those who hurt my birth father and his children. They did not win; my brothers and I won!

We have our lives—no guilt, no shame—regardless of all the challenges we've had to face. We still have love and kindness in our hearts. We have felt the hurt throughout our lives and know what it feels like. But we don't want revenge; let God take care of it!

Forgiveness is not easy, but it offers us huge rewards for our health, and it allows us to overcome bitterness, feelings of anger, and will bring peace for our inner selves. Forgiveness, as Scripture tells us, is essential: “Then came Peter to him, and said, Lord, how oft shall my brother sin against me, and I forgive him? till seven times? Jesus saith unto him, I say not unto thee, until seven times: but, until seventy times seven” (Matthew 18:21-22).

Chapter Three

The Shift/Revival

Although my parents divorced in 1964, my mother retained custody of us until 1967. That was the year she gave us, her children, up.

As I mentioned, the social upheavals of the 1960s occurred at different times in different places. In 1967, the counterculture was just reaching our part of the country. And though I haven't said much about Colorado, my heart remains there always.

Colorado is a Western state. The Rocky Mountains cover part of the state; much of the rest is on the Colorado plateau. The western edge of the Great Plains is also within the Colorado border. So the terrain is varied: it has some of the highest mountains in the lower forty-eight states as well as flat prairie. It's the only US state that lies entirely above one thousand feet in elevation. As a result, the air is a little thinner, and the cosmic rays are a little stronger (since there's less atmosphere to stop them). If you live there, it's nothing you'd notice, especially when you're young and healthy.

The word *Colorado* is one of the Spanish words for *red,* and the state was named by Spanish explorers after the Colorado River. The Spanish claimed it as part of their New Mexico province. The US acquired Colorado (and the adjacent states) as part of the Louisiana Purchase. The Spanish protested, but the issue was finally settled when Mexico gained its independence from Spain and the US won the Mexican-American War.

In 1849, prospectors came through en route to the California gold fields. Later, settlers bound for the fertile and lush Oregon territory passed through. Colorado remained a territory rather than a state for thirty-three years. One reason was uncertainty over whether Coloradans would vote to allow slavery in their state. When the vote was finally taken, they voted overwhelmingly to prohibit slavery. Curiously, those who voted *for* slavery tended to be former gold miners from the South. Although it is largely forgotten today, the first gold rush in the US took place in the Appalachians, primarily in Georgia. The expertise gained mining Georgian gold was instrumental to successful mining in California and other parts of the West—including

Colorado. That's how so many former southerners ended up in Colorado voting for slavery.

At first, Colorado attracted few settlers. Rainfall is sparse in much of the state. Native Americans claimed the land, and some of them violently opposed the influx of white settlers. Colorado marked the edge of fearsome tribes like the Apache and the Comanche. Local tribes like the Arapaho, the Cheyenne, and the Utes also attacked settlers.

After years of fighting, the Native Americans of Colorado were "pacified" and restricted to reservations by the US government. The most notorious conflict between whites and the indigenous tribes occurred in 1864, when a volunteer troop led by the Reverend John Chivington attacked a band of Arapaho and Cheyenne. Although they reported that they killed some five hundred warriors, members of the volunteers claimed that most of the dead were women and children. This is now known as the Sand Creek Massacre.

Colorado was finally admitted as a state in 1876, the 100th anniversary of the birth of the United States. For this reason, the state's nickname is "the Centennial State."

If Colorado had depended on attracting farmers and ranchers, its poor agricultural conditions would have kept its population small. Fortunately, like other Western states, Colorado has mineral resources worth exploiting. Colorado had modest resources of gold, but many major silver strikes occurred as well. The Colorado Silver Boom began in 1879 and continued for years. In the twentieth century, the state was found to be rich in petroleum. Uranium has also been mined in the state.

Today, tourism is also a huge industry, and the mountains are home to some famous ski areas such as Steamboat, Aspen, Telluride, and Vail. But it takes money and time off to ski.

Thus, I lived in an interesting state as a child. It was a place of dramatic vistas, sudden changes in the weather, and dry lands with little rain. I can understand why my father moved to Colorado from Minnesota with its harsh winters. Colorado also has a substantial military presence. So, as a wounded veteran, it was a good place for him to be.

And then there was my mother, Helen.

After the divorce, my birth father never married again—at least as far as I can tell. This wasn't the case with my mother. Her boyfriends were often around the house, but these relationships often seemed to end in acrimony. Usually there was a shouting match between my mother and her latest boyfriend, but it could sometimes turn violent.

I recall one incident when we lived in an apartment. My brothers and I were all home in bed with chicken pox. From my room, I heard one of my mother's boyfriends making her cry. I got out of bed, went up to him, and screamed at him to stop. I had no fear, and I had to protect my mother. I was used to this kind of behavior while living with my mother and her boyfriends. No child should have to be an adult.

We were always just scraping by. Many times, if I didn't have school, my mother took me to her place of employment. I had to sit quietly during her entire shift. I remember her standing at some sort of big machine that had tons of index cards coming down a conveyor system, and she pulled certain cards from the line. I watched her for hours.

Today, parents often schedule every waking moment of their child's life. When my brothers and I lived with my mother, we spent much of our time outdoors, unsupervised. But we also took long drives in my mother's light blue Volkswagen. One of those drives was in the mountains to a big brown lodge with a huge empty room. My brothers and I had to stay there, and we would play until my mother came back for us, which would make the time move faster. We would play hide and seek—there were many rooms to hide in—and I would also play with my doll.

I didn't have an ideal childhood, but neither did my mother, although it seems to have been a happy one. My maternal grandmother died in her fifties. One of my uncles—the youngest of my mother's brothers—died "in the war," which I took to mean World War II.

My mother had a picture in which she and her family appear happy. The only difference between me and Helen is that she had her family in her life. No one took her from her mother and father, and she was able to have a relationship with her parents.

After my mother broke off contact with us while we were in foster care, she married again. She even had another child, a girl named Margie. That marriage turned out no better. She left her second husband, much to his dismay. I've heard that he chased after her as she drove away in her pickup truck with Margie. Tragically, he later passed away.

Aside from missing my father, my life seemed normal until that night in 1967 when the police came and took my brothers and me away.

Chapter Four

After the Divorce

I am Elizabeth TroyLynn. But I'm also Troylynn Lindberg, as well as Troy Lynn. The latter is the name I was given at birth, when I was born in Denver, Colorado, on September 16, 1961, and I'll explain the rest in a bit.

After my birth parents divorced, my mother, my brothers, and I lived in several locations. The sequence of residences is mixed up in my mind, but I remember specific incidents. In the last home—the one from which we were taken by the police—we had a Saint Bernard named Charley, a dog that seemed impossibly huge when I was young. I so loved that dog! Charley was perhaps my only source of happiness during that season of my life.

One summer day, I remember Charley decided to pull me away from the fence at the edge of the property where I was playing. He dragged me away by my shirt, ripping it! Could my Saint Bernard have sensed some danger and been protecting me? I'm still grateful to that big beast! I miss Charley. Every time I see a Saint Bernard, I have such a great memory and hope that after we had to leave our home, he was well taken care of.

Other dogs were not so friendly. I recall a neighborhood German shepherd who lived up the street from my house. My brothers and I went to see the shepherd's new litter of puppies; she was on a bed in her owner's garage. I knew enough to not get too close, but although I stayed at the edge of the garage, she must have felt my fear and decided I was a danger to her puppies. She lunged and jumped on me and scratched my face. I came away from that encounter with a cut on one eyelid. My mother took me to an ER to treat it. I've been nervous around unfamiliar dogs ever since.

The disruption in our lives also meant I was not a particularly good student. The chaos of my home life did not lend itself to scholarship. To make matters worse, I had a speech impediment as a child. I lived in fear of being called upon to read out loud in class: I had a lisp and mispronounced words I didn't understand.

My uncertain home life ended that night in 1967 when the police took us to my mother's sister, Aunt Rachel. My aunt and uncle were at a much higher socioeconomic level. They took vacations! They had a boat! I kept thinking my mother would come back to take us to our home and that living with my aunt was only temporary, so I tried to enjoy the things I didn't have at home. I got to experience luxuries I'd never imagined. I learned to water ski! I went tubing on the water! There were new kids to play with in my aunt and uncle's very nice neighborhood.

Despite housing my aunt and uncle and their two boys, plus my two brothers, that house had enough space for me to have my own little bedroom in the back. I loved having my bedroom window open to the night breeze; it helped me sleep soundly.

When my brothers and I had been at my aunt and uncle's house for about a week, my mother showed up for a visit. This pattern was repeated a few more times. I fondly recall one such visit that my mother spent primarily with me. We sat in the kitchen alone and ate grilled cheese sandwiches with tomato soup. This is still one of my favorite meals! We ate and talked and had a wonderful time, but I wanted to go home with her and did not understand why she didn't take us.

As many people do, I associate memories with the senses. I remember the ones from that time period in this way:

Sight

- The house of Helen's sister, my aunt Rachel. I remember every room in that house. It seemed like such a big house to me. It had three bedrooms, a basement, and a nice backyard that I played in. I had my own bedroom upstairs, and it was decorated really fancily. I felt safe sleeping in that room.

- Going tubing on the water. While this engages many senses, the one that is unique to the situation is the sight memory. My brothers and I would go with my aunt Rachel and her family on the weekends. They had a boat. I remember falling off the tube into the water when we were going around the lake in the boat. Thank goodness I had a life vest on because I had no fear.

Smell

- I will never forget the smell of tomato soup. I have memories of my mother sipping tomato soup when we were together.

Sound

- The kids in the neighborhood made noise, and my mother spoke to me. I remember her voice as well as her words. And there was the horrid sound of my own speech defect. I struggled with pronunciation and would be embarrassed often.

Taste

- If I remember tomato soup from its smell, I recall grilled cheese sandwiches from their taste. I don't even recall what type of cheese it was, but I remember it didn't have much smell. It had a strong taste, though.

Touch

- Above all, I remember petting that huge, wonderful St. Bernard. Charley was so playful with me and was always looking after us. I remember he would sleep in my room some nights. He gave me so much happiness in that house.
- The boat and the water skiing engaged several senses. But the movement of the boat, the splashing of the water, were both primarily focused on touch. This was such a fun time for me. It helped me for a few hours to not think about the pain of not having my mother with me. Today I would call it natural therapy.
- And finally, the night breeze through the window in my bedroom, which helped me sleep.

We remember in different ways. Some memories engage one sense, others multiple senses. By identifying which sense is most engaged, we can fine-tune our memories. Some of my memories taught me to be thankful for what I had and that there was always hope.

If my brothers and I had grown up in that house, I'm not sure I'd have a story to tell. My aunt and uncle would have become my role models for a successful, peaceful family life. The chaos of the divorce and life with my mother seemed to be behind us.

But it didn't work out that way. One day, Social Services came for us. We were being placed with a new family. Our lives were being uprooted yet again.

Chapter Five

Damaged Goods

On their one and only visit to my family when we were young, my father's stepsisters found my birth mother's personality cold and off-putting. I later realized that my aunt Rachel had some of the same traits. Although my aunt would probably call her personality "pragmatic," the result was the same where my brothers and I were concerned: we had to go. My aunt just wasn't willing to take permanent responsibility for three additional children. I have no idea if my uncle wanted to keep us or if he simply went along with it. But one of them obviously called Social Services and asked that we be placed elsewhere. I suspect my aunt, angry at my mother for not getting herself together, made the call herself.

The new placement was a complete surprise to us. My brothers and I had felt safe with my aunt and uncle while my mother was at the hospital, and my aunt did not explain why we had to leave. She called us at our new foster home for a short time and then the calls stopped.

Our new foster family was not given much information about us. They were told that our father had died in the Korean War. And while it was true that my father was out of our lives for good, he wasn't dead.

Our new home was not far away in distance but a world away in attitude. Mr. and Mrs. Williams were very religious Baptists—he preached at the church nearby. The congregation was very supportive of all of us. For our very first Christmas with the Williams family, the church congregation chipped in and bought presents for each of us. Everyone was very kind. It was at this time in my life that I was introduced to God. I truly believe God has had angels watching over my brothers and me. There is no other answer.

I can still recall the day I was introduced to God. It was a crisp summer day at the foster home. My foster mother, Patricia Williams, took me outside to the front porch where we sat, and she told me a beautiful story about Jesus and how He loves my brothers and me. She explained that He was watching over us. Since then, this story from the Bible has always been in my heart. Before that day, I had never heard the story about Jesus; I had simply relied on my mother. It was like a transference of faith from my mother to God and Jesus. I put my faith in the story of Jesus. It was the only hope I had that my two brothers and I would be safe.

> *Excerpts from an August 2018 letter from foster mother Patricia Williams to Troylynn:*
>
> Christmas 1968 was a very special time. You three little crumb-crunchers were, like all kids, excited and in great anticipation! The social worker took you shopping so that you could each buy a gift for your mom, things for each other, and small things for all of us . . .
>
> We also helped you buy gifts for the kids in your class whose names you drew. (By the way, Troylynn, I still have the cute 10" decorated tree you bought for me. It's showing its age a bit, but I still put it out.)

Although the Williamses were very welcoming, I was hurt that my aunt and uncle did not want us. They called us on the phone for a short time, I think out of guilt. They seemed affluent enough to afford us, but we were not wanted. I was only six years old, but I already saw myself as damaged goods, unworthy of being around a "good" family. I felt that the Williamses were very nice, but I was still unsure if I could trust them. Would my brothers and I be there for a while, or would they give up on us too? It was sure a very scary time for me.

Many years later, I managed to get in touch with one of my cousins, my aunt Rachel's son. He had always been kind to me when we lived with them. His mother—my aunt—was still alive, and he put us in touch. Curiously, my aunt did not want a face-to-face meeting or a phone call. Instead, she communicated briefly via one email. Most of her email was the sort of thing you'd get in a Christmas card letter, just details about which family member did what. She insisted that she herself was doing quite well.

She has never explained why they turned us over to Social Services. I now understand that raising five children must have been quite a handful. She might have had a good reason: financial problems possibly, or illness. But by not giving us an explanation, she made us feel unwanted and unworthy of being part of her immediate family.

Did she feel guilty that they had turned me and my brothers over to Social Services? I have no idea. Her email and refusal to meet might have been a defense mechanism. Or she might have been completely oblivious to how we felt when we were taken away. Actions have consequences, but sometimes we refuse to accept responsibility for those consequences.

She did say something interesting in her email: she had met my father in the early days of my parents' relationship, and despite what Social Services had told the Williamses, he was still alive!

Excerpts from an August 2018 letter from foster mother Patricia Williams to Troylynn:

We had been fostering parents in Northglenn, Colo., for a while, but didn't keep track of how many children had stayed with us—some stayed for a day or two, some for a week or so—from babies up to teens. . . .

[In addition,] there were several years that we kept out-of-town teenagers who needed a place to stay in order to attend Silver State Baptist Christian School. There arose several problems in dealing with these kids, whose parents thought of the school as a reform school. Therefore, we decided to become foster parents of, hopefully, younger kids.

So, in October 1968, the social worker called to say that she was bringing three small children—two brothers and a sister. When she brought you kids, she said you'd probably be with us a few days. (SO glad she was wrong!) You brought your possessions in three large grocery-size brown paper bags. . . .

We weren't told much as to why you were placed in foster care. When you came into the house, your faces were somber and your eyes big with anxiety. We don't know if you had come right from your home or what, but I'm sure it was very perplexing as to why you were coming to stay with these total strangers. You looked like you were sweet little kids, but we didn't know what kind of "critters" you'd be. A couple of earlier foster kids (teens) had been difficult, for who knows what reasons. No telling what they had been through.

Chapter Six

New Beginnings

We were with the Williams family for three and a half years. Even though the Williams home was loving and pleasant, I still longed for my mother.

Excerpts from an August 2018 letter from foster mother Patricia Williams to Troylynn:

Troylynn, you liked having an upstairs bedroom all to yourself.

. . . you were so meticulous, polishing and re-polishing your furniture, arranging and re-arranging things . . . on top of the dressers. . . .

. . . as we soon discovered, you were all sweet, obedient kids. We may have had to get after you occasionally, but it appeared that your mother had raised you well. The social worker came about once a month to see how you were, and your mom was allowed a visit every month. Also, she could, and did, call you. I'm sure it was a very hard time for her. I can't imagine having your kids taken away. . . .

[At Christmastime in 1968] your mother accepted our invitation to come and stay overnight on Christmas Eve, and then be with you on Christmas Day. I remember it all being a very fun time.

In the family devotional time of reading the Christmas story from the Bible, we carefully explained to her (and you all, of course) that Christ came to earth to save lost sinners, and that we are all sinners. Then we explained . . . that if we'll confess our sins to Him ("for there is none good, no, not one;" "there is none that sinneth not.") and ask Him to save us from the penalty—which is to be cast into Hell for eternity; because he died for us, He will give us eternal life. We read to her from the book of Romans, Ch. 10:10 and 13: "For with the heart man believeth unto righteousness; and with the mouth confession is made unto salvation." "For whosoever shall call upon the name of the Lord shall be saved." There is no way we could ever pay for our own sins and merit heaven. If we could, then the Lord Jesus didn't need to die and shed His blood. He took our place.

How I wish I could tell you that your mom accepted Christ and His gift. She listened intently but didn't think she was ready to do that. It made us sad, but no one can "make" anyone else be saved. It's between the individual and the Lord, to whom they'll answer someday.

Well! What an exciting Christmas morning! All kids ran eagerly into the living room to find out what was in their piles of gifts! Your mom had brought gifts for you, packages had arrived from both sets of our parents, and we had things for you (and, of course, our children too). What excitement and laughter as you were handed gift after gift and ripped them open! (Oh, yes, the school principal and the teachers had sent you gifts as well.)

Finally, after quite a while of your ripping open one package after another, we came to the "bottom of the barrel." . . . Do you recall the picture we gave each of you which showed you three and your mother by our sofa, loaded down with all your new things? What a haul you made!

When my mother showed up for a Christmas visit, I excitedly thought that she was there to take us home. That, of course, did not happen. In fact, my birth mother's visits became rarer. Eventually, they stopped altogether, without even a goodbye. Much later, I found out that my mother's visits stopped because she had a new man in her life, and he didn't want her to be tied down by children.

Those are the exact words he used: *tied down*. To my mother's new boyfriend, my brothers and I were just an encumbrance.

The Williamses kept a big, happy home. They already had four children of their own. With the addition of my brothers and me, there were *seven* children running around!

Life with the Williamses centered on the family and their church. My brothers and I went with them to church several times a week (and always on Sunday). Going to church wasn't all fire and brimstone—the seven children got to play on the church grounds. There was a huge apple tree to climb, and we picked and ate the apples when they ripened.

Although the Williamses were not well off, we managed to take a vacation every summer. I recall our trip to Yellowstone Park as one of the best times in my life. It wasn't as much fun for Mr. and Mrs. Williams, as they fretted that one of the children would fall into a scalding-hot spring. At the time of our visit in the 1960s, there were very few guardrails in the park.

Excerpt from an August 2018 letter from foster mother Patricia Williams to Troylynn:

After a week or so, it became obvious that you didn't possess enough clothes, so a shopping trip was in order. You were thrilled with all your new things!

Day-to-day we didn't know if, or when, you might be leaving. After a year or less, we were all happy that it seemed permanent. Even so, by your mother's calls and visits we knew she felt desperate to get you back.

Right after you came, we enrolled you in Hulstroms Elementary School across the street from the parsonage, but we had enrolled two of our four kids in Christian schools, and we desired to place you in Christian school as well. We got permission from the social services and worked it out with Dr. Samson at Adams City Baptist Church and School that, starting in January, I would drive [a] bus and teach in exchange for your tuition. Very good of him! Learning to drive the stick shift van was, at first, terrorizing to me as I'd never driven such a vehicle—even on ice! I was responsible for a van-full of kids! Also, though I came from a line of teachers, I'd never taught anything but Sunday School. Well, we all survived, and I learned enough about teaching that I taught in Christian schools, off and on, for the next twenty years. You kids did very well and enjoyed school. [Mrs. Williams is being charitable—as I related earlier, I was never a good student.]

We also visited relatives of the Williamses. One of their relatives had a farm in Kansas, which afforded us with many, many adventures. That farm also provided the Williamses with enough meat to feed their large brood over the winter.

While we were visiting the farm, I got to ride the tractor, milk the cows, feed the chickens, and help with the canning, which made me feel so grown up!

Of course, children will find a way to fight about everything. On the farm it was usually the ants. My brothers loved to step on ants, and I felt obligated to protect them.

I am still in touch with the Williamses. I will always be grateful to them for taking us in and showing us what a loving family looked like. They are my role models and greatly impacted my life as they showed me there are good, caring people in this world. They were, and are, my angels! I will always love Mr. and Mrs. Williams with all my heart. Their children were always so kind to us and never made us feel like outcasts. But look at who their parents were! Mr. and Mrs. Williams led by example.

At last, it seemed as if my brothers and I were safe and secure. So, of course, it couldn't last.

Excerpts from an August 2018 letter from foster mother Patricia Williams to Troylynn:

For summer vacations, we usually went up to the Colorado mountains—mostly to Brush Creek—taking our old army tent and all the odd camping gear we had. There was hiking, fishing, exploring, ball games, and just relaxing in general. All [the] kids and the dog loved running and playing outside till you were happily exhausted. Food and sleep were always better in the Rockies! For some reason, food cooked over a campfire tastes better.

For one summer vacation, we rented a pop-up camper and had fun going to Yellowstone National Park. What a wonderful time! Our camping tent made a place for all the family to sleep. Apparently, we didn't camp where you—or any of us—would be in danger from bears or any other wild "animals." At least, we didn't seem able to get rid of any kids that way!

I don't know if you remember seeing some of those marvels there (in Yellowstone) which God created. Maybe you've been back there since that time. There were just paths to walk on going around the boiling mud "pots" and the little crystal-clear boiling ponds. One of them, they told us, was so hot that if animals fell in, they were quickly cooked. Believe-you-me, we were scared that we might head home minus a child. Some of us always held tight to your hands! (Never mind that our teenage boys would "play" threaten to throw you in!) . . . Brian and Keith took turns carrying you on their shoulders a lot of the time. I haven't found any pictures of us there, but surely some were taken.

Each of you found something at the gift shop, which you thought your mother would like. Anybody remember what they were? Soon after returning home, we had a birthday celebration for Victor the youngest brother, when your mother could come.

You all seemed to have a good visit with her; but it seems like it was after that visit that her visits and calls came less and less often. I don't believe it was because she didn't love you. About that time, the man she was seeing apparently didn't like for her to be "tied down" with children.

I guess we'll never really know what the circumstances were.

Chapter Seven

Wisdom from the Williamses

My brothers and I learned many things from Mr. and Mrs. Williams. With so many children—the three of us plus their own four—they had to organize their household carefully. They taught me the importance of sharing.

Dining, for example, was always a lesson in sharing. When a plate of food made its way around a table, it could easily be emptied if the diners did not share. Each person learned to take his or her share, and no more.

The meals were modest, but there was always enough. Our foster mother had learned how to stretch a dollar to feed us all. Meat at breakfast was a luxury and the bread was purchased when it was a day old, but none of us felt deprived.

Excerpt from a letter from foster mother Patricia Williams to Troylynn:

You were not selfish kids; however, it took some "larnin'" for you at our house. We, and of course our kids, were used to having to adjust our wants. For instance, when a bowl or plate of food was set on the table, everyone was accustomed to quietly dividing it into equal portions for however many people were around the table. It didn't take you three long to catch on, I think without our saying much about it.

I do remember, though, that when we went in November to my folks for Thanksgiving that when the platter of ham came around . . . it looked so good to Victor that he filled his plate with it. Mr. Williams, sitting beside him, said quietly, "Victor, you'll want other things on your plate, and maybe others will want ham." Victor put a lot back, and by the time we'd downed all the delish food, he was very glad he had put it back. One rule at our house was that everyone had to clean their plate.

One other item at this time of feeding nine or ten faces: it took a lot of bread for all the meals, plus making sandwiches every day for ten lunches. Once a week, the Wonder Bread Co. on 58th Avenue sold their day-old bread at ten [loaves] for $1.00. I'd go and buy thirty loaves, and we made it last a week.

Not only were the Williamses good to us but their parents were also. As a child, I didn't have the skills to recognize family dynamics. All I knew was that I felt as safe when I was with the Williams' parents as I did with the Williamses themselves. I also knew that the food was better when their parents were around.

Excerpts from an August 2018 letter from foster mother Patricia Williams to Troylynn:

We always tried to divide the holidays evenly between our two families: one on the farm in Kenney, Colorado, and the other at the Kansas farm of the Williams. Well, maybe I should say that we bugged them and mooched off them equally.

It was always a fun time to go to either farm—a chance to go "wild" as our kids would say. I don't know how much any of you remember about those times, but you were just considered as more grandchildren. I would imagine once you get past a certain number, it stops mattering in terms of hospitality.

My remembrance is that when you first came, there were a few times when your Aunt Rachel and/or Uncle William would pick you up and take you to, I believe, Boulder or Golden to visit with them and a grandma. After a short while your Aunt Rachel and Uncle William stopped coming.

My mom had died suddenly in 1963 at age 63, so when we went west to the Colorado farm, the food wasn't what it would have been. But all of us [the relatives] coming brought food, so there was lots of good stuff!

At the Williams' farm, everyone was stuffed to the gills! Grandma Williams would have ham and turkey and all the fixings. Then came desserts. She always "had" to have all kinds of pies and three or four kinds of cakes, Jell-O, whipped cream, and often homemade ice cream. We all brought food, too. Her homemade bread and rolls were wonderful!

So, you get the idea why everyone would be groaning when Grandma would say, "Now, let's all go into the living room and play and sing." Everyone was so full they could not move, but we all went and enjoyed it.

In the spring of 1970, Mr. Williams and I were privileged to be able to go to Israel with the teachers' group from Adams City Baptist Church and School, where you kids went. Grandma and Grandpa Williams graciously came to Denver to be with all you kids so we could go. When we arrived back home after two weeks, all seven kids seemed kind of sorry to see us, as you'd gotten so spoiled by all the delicious food!

Of course, the greatest gift the Williamses gave me was the gift of faith. I don't recall if my father was religious or not. He was out of our lives by the time I was five years old. However, I know that my mother was not religious. It wasn't something she talked about or exposed us to.

I look back today at the successes I have had in my life. I don't want to minimize my accomplishments, but ultimately, everything I have achieved is due to God. God is the reason I am still on this Earth. When I think of the impact I have had upon my own family, I remember that it was accomplished only by His grace, lots of hard work, and looking positively at each situation, even if it wasn't good.

Excerpt from an August 2018 letter from foster mother Patricia Williams to Troylynn:

Naturally, we always went to Sunday school and church. . . . You were all excited about going, and you were quick, eager learners. At that time, I was the teacher for the class that your brother Victor attended. Our lessons right then were about King David from the time of his herding his father's sheep, on to his slaying Goliath, to his friendship with Prince Jonathan, then Saul's jealousy, and Saul taking his soldiers to chase and try to kill David. All exciting adventures! Victor was on the edge of his chair; he didn't wait to be called on. He burst out, "Saul shouldn't chase him! Why didn't David just say, 'Cool it?'" We've laughed and laughed about that over the years.

Chapter Eight

The Court

Custody law varies from state to state. However, in all states, the welfare of children is taken into serious consideration. If a parent is considered unfit, the children may be taken away from that parent.

The Judicial Court of my region filed a "Petition in Dependency and Neglect of Children." Basically, the State wanted to end the custody rights of Helen, my birth mother. This would've been OK—after all, my mother no longer visited us—but it also changed our status in Colorado's child welfare system. If Helen's rights were voided, despite a successful three-and-a-half-year placement with the Williamses, we would be offered up for adoption.

That is exactly what happened.

> *Excerpt from an August 2018 letter from foster mother Patricia Williams to Troylynn:*
>
> We were blessed of the Lord to have you as part of our lives for as long as we did. And what a job and blessing to be able to know you as the great adults you've grown to be! Always stick together and love one another.

Despite everything, I would've been happy to go back to my mother. Staying with the Williamses, who loved us, would also have been a blessing. But the State had decided that we would have *yet another* family. This was so difficult, especially after such a long time being with the Williamses, who treated us like their own children.

On September 22, 1969, the court found the following:

- That the court had jurisdiction over the parties and the subject matter;
- That the children had been placed in foster home care by voluntary action of the mother;
- That the children were not domiciled with the mother;
- That the mother was currently unable to care for the children;
- That the parents were divorced.

The whereabouts of our father were unknown. Miss Larson was our caseworker for the local department of public welfare and gave her recommendations to the court.

The court sustained the petition:

- The children were adjudged dependent and neglected;
- Custody was given to the department of public welfare;
- A further hearing was scheduled for March 23, 1970. The court reserved the right to consider termination of the mother's parental rights.

So, we were in limbo until then. We continued to live with the Williamses during this time. I do know that the Williamses wanted to keep us forever, but the law back then would not allow this. I don't agree with this; our caseworker did not even ask us how we felt. Being with the Williamses for three years should have given us a right to have a say in what we wanted to the department of public welfare. I was so sad and scared during this time, not knowing where we were going next. What kind of people would they be?

When the next hearing came around, Helen was nowhere to be found. Usually it was my birth father whose whereabouts were unknown. This time it was my birth mother. Why didn't Helen show up for the hearing? My guess is because she had another child. But I'll get to that.

Helen was probably right not to show up visibly pregnant. The court was deciding if she were fit to retain custody of her children. And if she had shown up requesting custody of three children—children she had been unable to provide for, and pregnant with a fourth—she'd have sent a strong message that she was not capable of caring for any of us. As far as I know, she was unmarried at the time.

And yet, such is the bond between mother and child that if Helen had asked us to come back, my brothers and I would have immediately left the Williamses to return to live with her.

The court made its decision. Helen's parental rights to us were terminated. The court also ordered that an Alias Summons be issued, demanding that our father present himself to the court at 2:30 p.m. on May 18, 1970. Since his whereabouts were unknown, the Alias Summons was published in local newspapers. This was an attempt to draw my father out into the open.

Of course, my father never showed. But the State of Colorado couldn't have tried very hard. After all, my father was a disabled veteran receiving checks from the government. He was also still paying those auxiliary child benefits—the ones that should have gone to me and my brothers but were instead kept by my mother. And my father still had family in Minnesota who we could have gone to stay with, if they wanted to care for us.

So May 18 came and went with no sign of my father. The parental rights of my mother were officially terminated on May 23, 1970. I was nine years old. The court recommended that the parental rights of our father be terminated as well. My brothers and I were placed in the custody and legal guardianship of the director of our county's department of public welfare.

For the time being, we continued to live with the Williamses. But after the hearing on May 18, a caseworker began taking us out on visits to potential adoptive families. It was a very strange process, like auditioning for a new family.

Then, one day, the caseworker came and told Mr. and Mrs. Williams to pack our clothes. This time we would stay with our new family. This time we weren't coming back. I remember to this day walking out to our caseworker's car. I was not sure what was happening but knew something was not right, seeing our belongings coming with us. It was a very emotional time!

They didn't even allow us to say goodbye to Mr. and Mrs. Williams that day. A few months later we did get to see them one more time, but then Social Services cut off all contact. I don't agree with how they handled our case. Today you have what's called "an open adoption" that allows for some form of contact among the birth parents, the adoptive parents, and the children. This can also include pictures, letters, phone, or even intermediary or open contact. After being with the Williamses for the last three years, I considered them my new parents. The Williamses and my brothers should have been asked if we would want contact with one another, but that was not even asked.

Excerpt from an August 2018 letter from foster mother Patricia Williams to Troylynn:

After you were placed with your new family, your mom frantically and tearfully called us, over and over, begging us to tell her where you were. Our hearts went out to her, but, of course, we could not legally disclose this information to your mom of your whereabouts.

If you recall, your new family graciously invited all the Williamses to come for a lovely early Christmas dinner with you. Then we were told by social services to have no further contact.

It broke our hearts to lose our precious "little kids." But there was nothing we could do.

Chapter Nine

Adopted

Things were very different in 1970. The counterculture had reached Colorado. It was more than just fashion, like long hair and beards on men. Drug use reached every corner of the state. There was widespread rejection of authority. There were riots in many cities as well as mass protests.

Riots could break out for any reason. We were shocked when a riot broke out at halftime at a college basketball game in February 1970. But that is what happened when Brigham Young University played at Colorado State. At the time, the Mormon Church did not permit Black men to join the priesthood. Consequently, the Brigham Young University sports teams faced protests when they played away games. The blame was placed on CSU's Black Student Alliance, even though all the students who were arrested were white. Witnesses described the protest as peaceful until twenty riot police stormed the basketball court.

Some riots erupted out of protests against the Vietnam War. On May 1, there was a nationwide antiwar student protest. President Richard Nixon had just announced the expansion of the Vietnam conflict into the neighboring country of Cambodia. The protests escalated when, on May 4, poorly trained National Guardsmen opened fire on student protesters at Kent State University in Ohio. Four students were killed and ten injured by the guardsmen's bullets.

The women's movement was also gaining steam. August 26 was a designated Women's Strike for Equality. Nationwide events and protests were held. In most of the country, women could not have a bank account or credit card unless it was cosigned for by a man, usually the woman's father or husband. Of course, women were routinely paid far less than men for doing the same kind of work. If only that weren't still the case.

All in all, the United States was a very nervous country in 1970. No one knew how bad things were going to get. Many people seriously expected a revolution, with a violent overthrow of the government.

Back then, civil disturbance was usually political. Though there have certainly been shades of things like a potential violent overthrow of the government in recent months, like the January 6, 2021, insurrection at the US Capitol, nowadays more riots seem to come from parties that get out of control. When a major sports franchise wins the championship, the fans riot. The famous Red Rocks Amphitheater in Morrison, Colorado, used to be subject to riots at rock and roll shows, but the management has learned how to keep the audience under control.

Likewise, attitudes toward adoption have changed significantly as well. In 1970, the stance of the Department of Welfare was that it was psychologically better for children to make a clean break. I don't agree. I was sad for a long time that I didn't get to say goodbye to the Williamses. The way that our caseworker took us out of the home we had been in for the last three years so quickly without notice was so wrong! I do think that it is easier for the *caseworker* if the children don't get to say goodbye. How could one caseworker handle a houseful of wailing children who were clinging to their foster parents? I believe they are trained to show no emotion in the moment.

Once again, my brothers and I had a new family. The State mandated a trial period of two years, to make sure everything worked out. Then, on March 29, 1972, our adoption became final. I was eleven years old.

My adoptive parents asked me if I would be willing to change my name. Most children don't seem to like their names. I was an exception; I loved being Troy Lynn Lindberg. I knew my birth parents picked "Troy" while they were on a date at the movies. I wish now that I'd refused to change my name, but, as I keep reminding myself, we only have one life. I just wanted to make my new adoptive parents happy. I did not want to have to go to another new home. So I agreed to change my name.

I didn't realize it at the time, but there was an important reason that my adoptive parents pushed for my name change. By dropping Troy Lynn Lindberg, it made it much harder in those pre-internet days for my birth mother to find me. My adoptive parents didn't reveal this fact until I was much older.

My adoptive parents allowed me to pick my new name out of the Bible. I chose Elizabeth, which means "My God is bountiful: God of plenty." I had a new name: Elizabeth TroyLynn. The State of Colorado issued a new birth certificate for me with that name and my new parents' names. I also keep close to me my original birth certificate that has my birth name Troylynn. I have always felt growing up and still today this is who I am.

My new parents, the Andersons, could afford to buy me occasional presents—they didn't have to get help from a church. I recall getting a doll for my first Christmas with them; the doll was a darker color than me. I am so thankful they did this at such a very early age. It showed me that there are other beautiful colors in the world besides my own. I named my new doll Sasha. The Andersons made a wood crib and different outfits for Sasha. The Andersons only had one other child, a boy. So my brothers and I were part of a much smaller family than when we were with the Williamses.

I remember going on many camping trips with my new family in Black Hawk, Colorado. I always looked forward to going with our three Great Pyrenees dogs Aussie, Monte, and Beauregard. We got to sleep in tents and cook our food over the fire. I had this special place that I would go to all by myself; I felt like such a grown-up! It was a big rock that was right by a little cliff with the most amazing views of the mountain in the valley. I would sit on my rock in awe of the beautiful mountains. I would think about my life and where I wanted to go with it. It gave me so much peace. I do miss those days.

I also remember we would travel on weekends to a place I call paradise—Glenwood Springs. It's a little more than a two-hour drive from Denver. It is known for its hot springs and sits in the rugged Rocky Mountains, surrounded by the vast White River National Forest. Glenwood Canyon is rich with wildlife. The main reason we started going to Glenwood Springs was because, a few years prior, Victor started having issues with his Legg-Calvé-Perthes, a childhood disorder initiated by a disruption of blood flow to the head of the femur. He had to use crutches and then later had to wear a leg brace.

Native Americans called Glenwood Springs *Yampah*, which means "Big Medicine." There are fifteen minerals found in the water of the "World's Largest Hot Springs." Besides helping with aches and pains, soaking in the hot, highly concentrated mineral water has many health benefits. My little brother would soak in the hot springs, which really helped him as part of his treatment for pain. On cool nights, so much steam would rise off the pool that we could not see anyone in front of us! My brothers and I would play hide-and-seek in the pool. So much fun! I return to the mountains and Glenwood Springs whenever I can. To this day, I take my family back there. It has such a special place in my heart and tons of wonderful memories!

I am grateful for these memories the Andersons gave us. Our new brother, their son Jeremy, was very accepting of all of us. I have so much respect and love for my brother Jeremy. I must give the Andersons so much credit: adopting three children was quite a generous move. They kept me and my brothers together. Many people would not have done that. We came to them with a different past, uncertain and hurt, and they did their best to raise us.

But sometimes a person's best isn't enough.

I still had a lot of trouble in school. When we first came to the Andersons, my brothers and I were put into a Christian school for a very short time and then later moved to a public school. Mrs. Anderson told me years later that my teacher in the Christian school had told her I was dumb and had very little patience with me. The Andersons removed us quickly from that school. I am very thankful to them! Saying this about any child leaves a scar that will never go away. I had to forgive that teacher! Between my speech defect and being behind the rest of my class, I hated school.

When I was fifteen years old, I started acting out. Since I hated school, I cut class whenever I could. I wasn't doing anything sinister—I'd just leave campus and hang out in the park. I wasn't into drugs or alcohol. By not being in school, I would not have the teacher call on me to give an answer about what we were studying in class. I was extremely shy and did not want to be faced with giving the wrong answer or mispronouncing a word, feeling embarrassed in front of all my classmates.

I have gotten so much better over the years. I'm still shy but feel more comfortable with speaking up. From time to time I mispronounce a word, but I don't get as embarrassed as I did in school. It has taken a lot of hard, dedicated work, improving my speech by lots of reading and working with words, by sounding them out until I mastered how to correctly pronounce them. Giving up was not an option for me!

I also started sneaking out at night to hang out with my friends. We'd drive around and laugh, not doing anything in particular. I've always liked being with people who could make me laugh. Good medicine for the soul! Today as an adult, I see that this was not a good choice, sneaking out. Anything could have happened and ended with us never coming home again.

And like so many other adopted children, I obsessed about my birth parents—the couple I thought of as my "real" parents. I barely knew my birth father, but I desperately wanted to be reunited with him and Helen.

The Andersons were educated people. My adoptive father worked for the State of Colorado's Food Stamp program. My adoptive mother was a therapist. Since she was a trained counselor, she was usually the one who dealt with my misbehavior. It was a difficult time for all of us.

At that time in my life, I wanted people to like me; I was somewhat of a follower. So, when my school friend asked me if I would stash her beer and cigarettes until she came over the next day, I agreed to do as she asked.

Well, something happened that evening at home with one of my brothers. Victor was planning on running away so he took money from our adoptive parents. I asked why he was running away, and he said that it would be better for him and the issues he was dealing with, and he missed our birth parents. We talked about it, and I explained why that would not be a good solution for him because he was too young to go out into the world and make adult decisions, and why it would be best for him to stay put! Thank goodness he decided to stay. Also, after rethinking and deciding this was not a bright idea, my brother returned the money in order to do the right thing. I was not going to have my little brother leave and be by himself at such an early age. If he went, then I would have to go with him to make sure he would be OK. I had to ensure my brothers were going to be OK.

Shortly after my talk with Victor, our adoptive parents searched all our rooms, and guess what they found in my room? The beer and cigarettes I was holding for my friend.

I was truthful with them, but I was punished severely. In hindsight, as a parent, I too would have been worried about what my child was into, and I'd have wanted to get to the bottom of it.

But I didn't stop. The next week, my adoptive mom caught me sneaking out of the house at night. Being a therapist, she had connections. As punishment, she arranged for me to stay in a detention center for girls. This definitely got my attention. I was only there for one full day, but it was a stark warning of where my behavior could lead me.

The rules at the detention center were strict. I had to surrender my belt and shoes, and I was put in a tiny bedroom. Worst of all, I was always under surveillance. I was *so* relieved when Mrs. Anderson came and got me out! That harsh lesson worked. I changed my behavior . . . if only insofar as making sure I didn't get caught. I remember coming home afterwards, and I still had a lot of proving to do, so my adoptive parents had me sleep on the floor of their bedroom each night for about a month. Honestly, I was not upset about it and did what I had to do to prove that I would never sneak out again. I never did again and stayed out of trouble! I am so thankful to Mrs. Anderson for what she did to help me to stay on the right path.

Although life became more settled for a while, change is inevitable. As the years passed, the relationship between my adoptive parents deteriorated. I won't pretend to understand what the problem was. We were never told. But it ended up with them getting a divorce. Mrs. Anderson moved out, leaving us children with my adoptive father.

I recall phoning my adoptive mother and asking if I could come live with her. I was devastated when she said no. She told me that she was working out of her home as a therapist and building a client base, and I would only be in the way. I just wanted to feel loved and wanted by my adoptive mother. As a mother today, I could never have rejected any of my children. It would have been a yes from me have my daughter live with me, and we would make it work.

In the end, however, I did have to respect Mrs. Anderson's decision, whether I agreed or not. People make decisions for their own reasons, and we may not always know the entire story. But, once again, I felt completely rejected. Whether it was true or not, I felt as though I had been rejected by almost every parental figure I'd ever had.

My birth mother had taken me away from my father. The record shows that my mother attended a court hearing on September 22, 1969. It's clear that she did not want to disclose that my father was a disabled veteran and had been receiving checks from the government. He could have been found, and I will always question why she would not disclose this information to the courts. Was she protecting herself, trying to keep my father from learning about what she did? Why did she not want us to go to my biological father and his family if she could not care for us? It seems selfish to me. My birth mother was able to stay with her own family; no one came and took her away from them. So why did she not give me and my brothers the same courtesy?

My aunt and uncle—who took care of us after our mother was taken away—rejected me and put me in the system.

And then my adoptive mother rejected me! I lived with my adoptive father, but we didn't interact much. He was going through his own issues from the divorce.

The only parents who had not rejected me were the Williamses, and the State of Colorado had forced them to give up custody. I felt like the girl no one wanted. I might as well have had the word *unwanted* tattooed on my forehead.

Chapter Ten

My First Love

By tenth grade, I just wanted out of my situation. I felt rejected at home. I was miserable in school—always behind, always embarrassed. My failures in school made me feel stupid and worthless.

I started begging my adoptive parents to allow me to quit school and enter the workforce. At the age of sixteen, I was old enough to leave school, but only with their permission. After a month of begging them to let me quit, they finally gave in. In retrospect, I'm surprised that two educated, professional people would allow their sixteen-year-old to leave school. Were they giving up on me or were they trying to give me what they thought I wanted? Perhaps they were just caught up in their own problems dealing with their contested divorce. They finally signed the papers that allowed me to quit high school.

Whatever the reasons, I now feel like my foster parents let me down. They were the adults, after all. They were professional people who knew the value of an education. Why didn't they get me the help I needed? I needed tutoring. I needed a speech therapist. After all, my adoptive mother was in the "help business" as a counselor! Instead, they gave up on me and let me do what I wanted.

Or could this have been the pathway I was supposed to be on? One that would prepare me for what was to come? I will always have love and respect for my adoptive parents for everything they did for me. They did the best job they could with all the added responsibility. Unfortunately, they have both passed away.

At seventeen, I met my first boyfriend, Richard, through my best friend and quickly fell in love with him. It's not surprising that I fell so hard, so fast, after feeling rejected by so many people in my life. To find someone that I loved, who loved me, and who would never reject me . . . that's exactly what I wanted.

We dated for a year. Then we moved in together. And, at the age of eighteen, we got married. My adoptive father walked me down the aisle. We had a beautiful small ceremony at the church that Richard and I attended every Sunday. My brothers, cousins, and friends were also in attendance.

The only disappointment was that my adoptive mother was not there—not even for the preparations. I got word from my adoptive father that she wasn't feeling well, but this was just another example of her letting me down during this time. I felt disappointed because I was really looking forward to spending time together and getting her input about the perfect dress.

It was already hard enough knowing that my birth parents would never see this special day of their daughter walking down the aisle. I truly wanted my adoptive mother there, but she did not even let me know personally that she could not make my wedding or the preparations, and that's what hurt so much. I do not know to this day why this happened. After the wedding, she didn't ask me any questions about the ceremony, and I eventually had to let it go. I refused to let her absence ruin my wedding.

It wasn't as if I wanted my adoptive parents to spend a lot of money on the wedding. I wanted things practical, simple, and efficient, so there was no bridal shower. I had come up with another plan for the dress. Thankfully Sandy, Richard's sister, offered to let me wear her own wedding dress. I will always be grateful for Sandy's help during this time—she was a great sister-in-law!

Our reception was held at my new in-laws' house. I was so grateful for those people who really made my day so special!

It started off so well. After the lovely wedding, my husband and I settled into our new lives. Employment was strong in 1979, and it was easy to get a mortgage. My husband was in construction, and he had as much work as he could handle. I worked in a nursing home for two years, which was gratifying even though the pay was low. I switched to the service industry and became a waitress at the age of twenty. I was lucky in my place of employment. The restaurant where I worked was frequented by the Denver Broncos, who were then under Coach Dan Reeves. Their presence brought many other people into the restaurant. I was hired as a hostess and then promoted to a waitress and was able to make a little more money. My tips were usually good, and it was a fun environment in which to work.

The American dream seemed to be working out for my husband and me. We had jobs, a nice car, and even a small house. The mortgage was $345 a month. We went to church regularly. Life was good and promised to get even better.

But we also had responsibilities to our relatives. My husband's grandmother became very ill and needed someone to care for her. My husband's father asked us to be her caregivers. After some discussion, we agreed. We rented out our home and moved in with my grandmother-in-law in Nebraska.

Politically, Colorado has historically been a "purple" state: both liberal *and* conservative. Whatever your political beliefs, you can find other people in Colorado who agree with you. Nebraska is a different story. Colorado is historically a mining and ranching state. Today, its economy has diversified. Tourism is a big part of the state's economy. But Nebraska? Nebraska is a farming state, and farmers tend to be very conservative and very Republican. I don't know why. There are entire books written on the subject. But if any place escaped the dislocations of the counterculture of the '60s and '70s, it was Nebraska.

But Granny was a kind ninety-five-year-old woman. To this day I consider it a blessed honor to have taken care of her. She was such a nice person; my joy was keeping her house inside and out. I enjoyed our talks and always wanted her to feel loved. My husband and I still needed to bring in an income, so we took care of Granny in shifts. This meant that my husband and I saw less and less of each other because when one of us was home with Granny, the other was out working. We did not have a lot of spare time to go out and do things; it was a super busy time for us.

Our sojourn in Nebraska lasted about a year. Eventually, Granny deteriorated beyond our ability to take care of her, and she had to go into a professional care facility. My father-in-law found a very nice nursing home and moved nearby, as he had retired. My husband and I moved back to Colorado. And that's when the trouble began.

Chapter Eleven

Homecoming

Until we moved back from Nebraska, my husband and I rarely drank alcohol. But once we returned to Colorado, my husband's new place of employment had him traveling weekly to Steamboat Springs, and our time together was only on Fridays and Saturdays. He was stressed about the amount of work travel and started to drink.

Something was changing in his personality. His anger came at me in bursts. He would have outbursts for no apparent reason. To this day I'm not sure how this change came over him. Was it just the drinking? All I knew was that, for the first time, I began to fear my beloved husband.

After about six months of this behavior, he started to withdraw from me and eventually asked for a divorce.

I thought he had met someone else on one of his nights out while traveling for work. I did everything in my power to help us and our marriage, but he wanted out and never gave me a reason why. I loved him with all my heart! Years later, I did learn there was not another woman; he simply did not want the responsibilities that came with a marriage, like a mortgage and bills. Being an adult.

I realized as I got older that some couples who get married at such a young age can feel as if they have missed out on an entire stage of their life, which can lead them into being very unhappy. But at the same time some young marriages have lasted many years and the couple is still very much in love.

I have no regrets. As I look back now, I have no doubt I was meant to be on this pathway, one not of my choosing, in order to prepare me for bigger things to come. To strengthen me. And I had to trust that God was in my life. As Scripture tells us, "Trust in the Lord with all thine heart; and lean not unto thine own understanding" (Proverbs 3:5).

He wanted out and filed for divorce. Once again, I was devastated. I had gone through so many rejections with my birth parents and foster families, but I thought I had put that behind me when I became an adult and started my own family. I was wrong.

To make matters worse, the economics of the divorce were in my husband's favor. He was a construction worker at a time and place where his skills were in high demand. I was a waitress and an unskilled health care worker. My husband was the one who made a good living. I couldn't even support myself on my income.

I sought advice from my adoptive father, but he had little to say. He had remarried and was starting a new family. I was in his past, and I got the impression from our conversations that he did not want to be bothered. I had to figure out what to do alone.

At a loss, I allowed my husband to convince me to meet with *his* divorce attorney. That attorney did exactly what you would expect: he looked after the best interests of his client, my soon-to-be ex-husband. My former in-laws took over the mortgage on our little dream house. They allowed my ex-husband to stay there. He was the one who wanted out while I contributed to the house with my income, and yet I was the one who had to leave. I was out on my own, with no place to live and low-paying employment. Unable to afford the payments, I even had to give up my car.

I might have become homeless were it not for Emma, my best friend from middle school. She was renting a house and allowed me to move in with her. I am ever so grateful for her kindness and help, and for loving me in one of my worst moments. I took whatever work I could get, holding down multiple jobs at the same time. But, without even a high school diploma, the only jobs I could get were low paying.

I have seen people seem to come to a point where they have flashbacks of their lives. They start to see everyone they have hurt in their journey, and they understand how they've treated people. Some make it right with the ones they've hurt, and some don't. Recently, I heard from my first love, Richard, now my ex. He found me on Facebook. He told me that since he left me many years ago, he has never found happiness. He has always been climbing mountains, searching for something different. He spent all those years trying to find it and never did. He was so sorry that he hurt me, that I was his only true, real love, and he blew it.

It's too late now forty-some years later, but I told him the challenges I had to face as a result of his choice. He told me his family was very upset at what he had done to me and that they loved me so much. I had a great relationship with all of them. When Richard left, I was hurt and ashamed that I could not make my marriage work. I thought I was a failure to have to say goodbye to them. I wish now I had talked to them and told them my side of the story. But we are both forty years too late.

We all must live with the choices we make in this one life we have, especially when we hurt people. While I have forgiven Richard and want him to be happy, we cannot rewrite the past. A big part of me will always care. Forgiveness is so important to allow love to prosper in your life. There is a story, a journey behind everyone. There is a lot of goodness inside of him. I saw it many years earlier when I had become quite ill.

Soon after Richard and I married, I developed Guillain-Barré syndrome, which is a rare disorder in which the body's immune system attacks the nerves. There's no known cure for Guillain-Barré syndrome, but several treatments can ease symptoms and reduce the duration of the illness. Although most people recover, the mortality rate is between 4 percent and 7 percent. Between 60 to 80 percent of people are able to walk at six months. I was in the hospital for about two weeks. It took close to a year to fully recover, and even today I sometimes experience muscle weakness. Richard was the only one who was there for me and helped me each day to get better. Thank goodness, I made a full recovery! I will never forget what Richard did for me during that time.

Eventually, after the divorce, I found a full-time job that filled my needs. I went to work as a leasing agent in a large apartment complex. That job also gave me a discount on an apartment, so I could live in a decent place once again. I worked very hard and was a good team player. I showed up for work every day with a good attitude. Part of my responsibilities was doing the bookkeeping for tenants' accounts and renting out apartments. This made me feel more self-confident. I was horrible at math in my early years, and I had to study hard to get better, but this job proved I could do it!

I worked my way up the ladder in the leasing business. In 1986, my good friend Ava got me a job as her assistant at a very large, upscale apartment community. I became the assistant manager. The job included great incentives, including very low rent on a beautiful home. As assistant manager, I finally had the income to buy nice furniture for my place. I even fulfilled a longtime dream of mine and bought a Camaro! I was grateful for this opportunity and worked hard to show my appreciation. I will always be so grateful to Ava for what she did for me. For believing in me! I even went to night school classes through the high school that I attended for a short time many years ago to earn my GED. My confidence was finally starting to grow .

While I was working several odd jobs, I had no time for dating or socializing. But once I had a well-paying job, my evenings were free again. Ava and I went out dancing often, which is something that I have always loved and done well. During the more stable periods of my childhood, I had gotten to take tap and jazz dance lessons.

One night at a dance club, I spotted a young man who was a very good dancer. He could dance like Michael Jackson. Believe me, he had the moves! He approached me and we talked, and it turned out that he was looking for a dance partner for a national televised competition. We began practicing after work several nights a week, and a friendship grew between us.

The dance competition was fun but also scary. I had never been filmed before, and the cameras felt very intrusive. We danced our hearts out and did very well. In the end, we didn't win; we took second place. Even so, I was very proud of myself!

After the competition, my dance partner inserted himself into my life. He would come over uninvited, insisting that we hang out. I wanted to be friends with him but nothing more. That's not the way he saw it. He would show up at my house uninvited and kept showering me with praise, adoration, and attention. He would say things like "I love you" and "I can't live without you." He was very persistent and kept pushing me for a relationship. What really sucked me in was that he said he was a Christian and a churchgoer. Growing up in the church in the Williamses' home, this was an important quality for someone in my life to have. He invited me to the church that he had been going to for some time. I accepted members of the congregation as friends, loved the preacher, and felt very comfortable in that church.

After a few months, I finally gave in and entered into a relationship with him. He soon started showing up at my job with flowers. He would call me minutes before I got off work to confirm what time I would leave so we could hang out. After a few months, I started to believe he had a very kind heart! Unfortunately, I would soon learn otherwise.

This was Summer 1987. Things seemed to be going well. I had a pretty good job that paid the bills with a little money left over. Our relationship started to bloom, but not long into the relationship things started to change.

One of the first times his aggressive behavior manifested was when he called my work and invited me to dinner at his home. I agreed but told him it was a very busy day with a lot of clients coming in, and I would be working a little late. He said that would be fine, and he'd see me later. Shortly after arriving at his house that evening, he started asking me tons of questions about why I had to work late and whom I had been with. When I answered, he said he didn't believe me. I started to feel very uncomfortable and told him I wanted to leave. He grabbed me and pushed me back from the door, saying that I was not going to leave. I did not know what had happened, and I wanted to get out of his house. I was shocked by his behavior.

Then he did something truly bizarre. He gave me a broom and told me to hold it in the air; if I dropped it, I would not be allowed to leave! I thought he was playing around, but soon realized it wasn't a joke. Frightened, I did what he demanded: I held the broom up in the air and when I became tired and let the broom down, he became very angry with me. I thought he was going to hit me. After a few minutes, he took the broom back and said he'd been kidding. Some hours later, he allowed me to leave, but only after he explained why he did what he did and that he was sorry. As is common among abusers, he told me that I had to convince him that I still wanted to be in a relationship with him. He demanded that I declare that I loved him more than anything.

With all the rejection in my life, I would do almost anything not to feel that again. I acceded to his demands. I had never seen this type of behavior before, so I had no idea of what it would lead to. I was so vulnerable. He knew how to detect my weak spots. He used my vulnerability and past pain to take advantage of the situation. Playing on my fear of rejection, he made me feel like I was 100 percent loved.

This man was extremely intelligent. He never drank alcohol, smoked, or used any drugs. That was one of the things I most liked about him. I didn't want a relationship with someone using alcohol or substances of any kind. Shortly after the incident with the broom, he started showing up more than usual at my house and my job. He would say hi to my boss and coworkers, trying to insert himself into my work life. Seeing that I'd become hesitant to be alone with him, he put on the charm even more. Inexperienced as I was, I had a hard time interpreting this behavior.

So I gave in. I think if I'd had a good support system, a family who could help me, then I could have seen the danger signs and walked away. But the only fully supportive family I'd ever experienced were the Williamses, and the state took me away from them.

There are thirteen traits common to abusers. My boyfriend at that time had all these traits. I still remember all of them and their connection with his personality.

1. Charming
2. Jealous
3. Manipulative
4. Controlling
5. Victimizer
6. Narcissistic
7. Inconsistent
8. Critical
9. Disconnected
10. Hypersensitive
11. Vicious
12. Cruel

13. Insincerely repentant

Domestic or dating violence is a pattern of controlling behaviors that one partner uses to get power over the other. It includes physical violence or the threat of physical violence to get control, emotional or mental abuse, and sexual abuse.

Leaving isn't as easy as it seems. Domestic violence survivors are often asked why they didn't leave. But consider this: How would you feel about leaving your partner? As difficult as it may be to admit, in domestic violence relationships, abusers have often put the victims in a position of being dependent on them on many levels—including financially—to keep them from leaving. Programs designed to help victims leave must address these concerns.

Perhaps most important, though, is the fact that leaving can be dangerous. Research consistently shows that abusers are more likely to kill their victims in the two weeks after they leave than at any other time. When considered in conjunction with the fact that leaving can spark financial troubles, not to mention the pain of losing a relationship, it becomes easier to understand why so many survivors are hesitant to leave.

I didn't know how to get out of it. I really thought it was love! The chronic abuse started with name-calling, telling me how to dress, and determining who I could talk to. He had a rationale for his behavior, saying, "I do this because I love you so much," and "No other man will love you like I do." Absurdly, I started to believe it! In the beginning, I could always seem to calm him down after each outburst. I learned what words to use to make him calm, the phrases that made him feel important, powerful, and like the good guy. I wasn't just walking on eggshells around him, I was soon walking through a minefield. My entire world started to revolve around him. Over the next two years, I was constantly afraid of taking a wrong step, which would incite his rage.

We started to attend a small new church every Sunday and during the week. We became very involved in church social events. We even met some great people who turned into friends. When I was in church, I felt happy, content, and safe. Having a family and feeling loved was very important for me. The church gave me that. But soon, he started viewing other men in church as a threat to our relationship. He accused me of flirting with everyone around us. "I know you're looking at him," he would say. He started to want to know my every move and would not allow me to go to church without him.

By then, his mood swings were obvious: one minute he was happy and the next he'd be furious. He would think nothing about degrading or verbally attacking me in front of people. While attending a prayer meeting one Wednesday, he said in front of the entire audience that our pastor should pray for me to be a better woman for him. It was so difficult to hear, and I was embarrassed. My pastor, Bishop Leonard, sternly told him that he should not degrade me but should instead raise me up. While I was happy that the pastor had said something, I was also scared that this would incite another outburst when no one was around. Sure enough, after we left the church, he insisted that our problems were my fault. He called me stupid and ugly, asserting that no man would ever want me.

Then the real physical abuse started. That same day after church and the incident after arriving home, he threw me to the ground and put his hands on my neck and started to choke me. I couldn't breathe and didn't know how to get out of it. I was lucky he didn't kill me then and there.

He insisted that I was not allowed to call my family. All I needed was him, he maintained. He started isolating me from them through fear and violence. As punishment for calling my little brother one Saturday morning, he gave me a black eye! He warned me that next time would be even worse. My brothers had no idea what was really going on, and I was scared to tell them for fear of getting hurt again. I wanted to get out, but I was terrified that if I left, he would surely find me. In the beginning of our relationship he told me he had been in the military and was trained to track the enemy. How could I ever get away from someone who could find me wherever I went?

Abuse became an almost weekly event. I always had bruises on parts of my body. Eventually, I had to leave my job. I'd loved working there, but he insisted that I find a job that he approved of.

I finally got another job at a different apartment complex. This was more acceptable to him because I was not working with my friend, and I was therefore more isolated. I worked as a leasing agent and cleaned apartments. Again, I received low rent as part of my compensation package. I really liked my new boss and looked forward to going to work every day.

One day after about four months into the job, I was out on the property with the maintenance staff addressing an issue. At the end of my shift, I walked home. We lived on site, not far from the rental office. Shortly after I arrived home, my boyfriend asked me whom I'd been speaking to. His interrogation was extensive, which made me think he'd come home early and watched me from the house. After about thirty minutes of this, he dragged me into the bedroom where no one would hear us. He kept shaking me and choked me to the point I passed out. I have no idea how long I was unconscious, but when I came to, everything was so cloudy it was as if I were in a dream. Even he was shocked by his violence; he was crying and saying how sorry he was. But of course, he felt it was all my fault for making him angry. To keep him from getting violent again, I told him that I loved him and that I had deserved it. Soon I was crying too—although my tears were from fear and wishing I had a family that could help me get away from him.

I had to find a way out. I couldn't tell my boss what was going on. I was scared he would fire me. I knew that if my neighbors heard the violence going on and complained, I would be let go. I needed to get out of this isolation.

It was such a terrifying position to be in!

The only career I knew at that time was the apartment business, but I knew I could quickly land a job because of my experience. I had to get a different job, because I was so afraid that my boss, whom I really liked, would soon discover what was going on because one of the tenants complained of the abuse, and he would have to fire me. If I kept getting fired for this reason it would soon be harder for me to land a new job. I worked hard and always had such positive feedback from my managers, but once again I also had to find a job that my abuser approved of. And in order to keep my new job, I had to agree with him that he would take the car keys. After all, I worked in the apartment complex, so there was no place I had to drive.

Time went by. Some days were good, but some were very, very bad. I kept telling myself he would change and that he really loved me. One night, he said he would take me out on a date. He knew I loved to dance, so we went to dinner and then to a dance club. While we were out, I ran into an old girlfriend whom I had not seen in a long time. I introduced them and he seemed OK with her. At the end of the night, she asked me to meet for lunch and we set up a date. To my surprise, he had no problem with me having lunch with her. I was so happy!

However, as the day for my lunch date approached, he became jealous and tried to discourage me from meeting with her. I assured him that I would only be an hour and he would know where I was. He agreed if he could drive me.

On the day of the lunch, he was acting very strange. From the time we got up, he said he was very depressed and did not want to be alone. But I had a plan—I was going to finally tell someone. I would tell my friend what was going on and seek her advice.

There are three phases of domestic abuse. The honeymoon phase is when everything is going great. Then the tension builds, leading to a violent incident. My boyfriend was always so remorseful after inflicting violence and promised he would change. This cycle makes it difficult to break free from an abusive partner. I'm not sure how I did it, but I talked him into letting me go to lunch with my friend, and even got permission for her to pick me up. I had a very uneasy feeling in my gut that day, but it was so refreshing to see my longtime friend. During our conversation, I finally broke down and told her everything. I showed her the fresh bruises I had while looking out the restaurant window to make sure he wasn't sitting in his car watching me. My friend was horrified and insisted that I could not go back. But I had left my personal items back in the apartment with him including my driver's license, car keys, checkbook, and my birth certificate. All the things I needed were in that house. I think back now and realize that I should have had a backup of all my personal items outside of our home. Then I wouldn't have had to go back.

We came up with a plan. When I arrived home, she would stay in the car and wait. I would tell him that my friend wanted to borrow a dress for a function, and I would grab something from my closet and take it out to her. If I didn't come back out to her in ten minutes, she was going to call the police.

Upon entering the house, I got an eerie feeling. All the lights were off, and the curtains were pulled shut. It felt very cold. As I walked to the bedroom, I called out his name. He mumbled. When I entered the bedroom, I saw he was in bed. It was very unusual for him to be sleeping in the early part of the day. Something was wrong.

My heart raced as I spotted a shotgun sitting in the corner by the bed. He'd never had any guns. Where did this come from and why was it in our house? How was I going to convince him to let me go outside to my girlfriend's car? He stirred a bit. He looked at me and ordered me to get into bed. He talked funny, as if he were on medicine that made him sleepy. Was he on something? I told him my girlfriend was waiting outside to borrow a dress and I had to run it out to her. I moved things around as if I were looking for the dress and managed to get my birth certificate hidden inside of it. I had to grab my car keys from the kitchen, then go to the living room without him knowing. He was still very quiet and hadn't made a peep. After leaving through the front door, I felt such fear with every step. I made it to her car. I knew that he could come out at any moment, the shotgun in his arms. If that happened, I knew he would kill me, and perhaps my girlfriend, too.

It seemed to take forever to get into my girlfriend's car. We sped off as soon as I was inside. The plan was for me to stay with her for a while, which worried me. I knew that his military training had taught him how to find people. His oldest brother was also in the Army and had told me stories in the beginning of our relationship about my boyfriend's training.

Shortly after we got to her place, I called the police to inform them about the gun and his condition. They asked me to meet them back at the house to let them in. I was hesitant, but eventually agreed.

Arriving at the house, I gave the police the keys so they could enter. Soon I heard sirens. As I was waiting outside, more police and an ambulance showed up. Everyone rushed inside. It seemed to take forever, but I finally saw them bring him out on a stretcher and take him away. The police said they found an empty pill bottle in the covers. They suspected his plan was to go to sleep after he shot me. This was sick, horrible, my stomach hurt so bad! How had I gotten myself into this mess? Surely, someone was watching over me. I was able to get my most important possessions out of the house but left everything else. He could have it. It was not important to me. I knew that I had to quit my job and move right away. I never wanted to see him again.

I soon found another job in the apartment leasing community far away from him in a different county. It was the beginning of 1987. Life was starting to calm down. I continued to work hard at my job and attended another church every Sunday. But it was too good to last.

Chapter Twelve

A Miracle on the Way

One Sunday, while at church, I was talking to some girlfriends in the lobby. Suddenly my ex was there smiling at me! My heart started pounding a mile a minute. How had he found me? I worried about causing a scene in front of my new church family. They knew nothing about my troubled relationship. In order not to upset him, I smiled back, which was the wrong thing to do. That smile opened the door once again.

We talked for about an hour and agreed to go have coffee. I drove my own car; being alone with him in a car would have been too uncomfortable. He seemed different, more relaxed. But I was on edge. Think back on my list of the thirteen traits common to abusers: this day he was *Charming, Manipulative, Victimizer.* If you have never been in this type of relationship, it's hard to understand what the abuser does to deceive and cleverly draw his target in time after time. Abusers try to sway your emotions and make you feel irrational and more likely to give in to their requests. You start to believe that they have changed.

Once again, over the next few months, the pattern repeated itself. We went from being friends to being in a relationship. Soon after, his aggressive behavior resurfaced. This time he began hitting my body where no one would see. His attitude hadn't changed: he said he owned me. I was his property. As before, I would take it and hope that I would come out OK.

The stress led me to starting to smoke at work. One day he found a cigarette in my purse. I was given another black eye for this. He was against any form of substance abuse (apparently, the sleeping pills the police took from him didn't count), so he found the cigarettes to be unforgivable. Then he made me have dinner with him in a restaurant with a black eye. I remember all the people looking at me and then at him with disgust—but no one helped me, not one person. He looked with such joy at this public domination of me. Afterwards, he warned me that he would do it again if I didn't follow his rules.

A few months later, I decided I had to end this. I took a big chance and broke up with him, calling him from my job. This was a risk since he knew where I worked and also where I lived. But it couldn't go on: I weighed around ninety-nine pounds, was run-down, and was sick all the time. What did I have to lose?

Surprisingly, he didn't immediately confront me. Several weeks went by, and I didn't hear a peep from him. I was scared all the time, expecting him to show up. I was always looking over my shoulder. I felt that he was doing this on purpose to keep me scared.

One evening I arrived home after running errands. Walking up to my home, I saw a piece of paper taped to the door. I put my bags down and opened the letter. It was from my girlfriend, who had helped me another time, who now was also my boss. The note said that she'd received an after-hours emergency call from an unknown caller that "they" needed to check my apartment because I was threatening to kill myself. My girlfriend was in a panic and called the police. She opened my apartment, and the police went in, thinking they were going to find me dead. Of course, there was no one inside . . . but all my furniture was gone! There was no one else in my life who would have made this call; I knew it had been my ex. I believe he took my furniture as a means of economic abuse so that I would have to depend on him again since I had nothing.

In addition to my furniture being gone, the place was a mess. Because of my low income and frequent moves, I didn't have many possessions. Nevertheless, the invasion was traumatic. I didn't sleep at all for fear the thief—my abuser—would come back. He had gotten in through a window by my front door. I had a pretty good feeling I knew who was responsible. After all, an ordinary thief wouldn't have told my friend that I was going to kill myself.

The next morning, I got up and intended to go straight to the police. However, as I approached my car, I saw some black stuff on my car windows. I froze: what was it? When I opened my car, it smelled strongly of gasoline. It appeared that someone had tried to set my car on fire! Apparently, they'd failed since the fire left only a sooty residue on the windows. I was scared to drive the car for fear of it exploding with me in it. I went back into my apartment and called the police. Now I was sure who the culprit was, but I couldn't prove it.

Because of this incident, I was asked to leave my job. Apartment complexes have enough difficulty with tenants who cause problems—they don't allow an employee to stay if that employee causes problems (even if it isn't the fault of the employee herself). Thank goodness that the laws have changed since then and there is more protection against being evicted from your home.

My girlfriend couldn't keep me from being fired, but she helped me get another job far away. I was not angry with her; she was very kind throughout my ordeal. I understood that I had to leave for my own safety, as well as for the safety of the other residents who lived there.

According to the Centers for Disease Control, in the United States, nearly twenty-four people per minute are physically abused by an intimate partner. This equates to more than ten million people each year. This kind of crime accounts for approximately 15 percent of all violent crimes. Seventy-seven percent of domestic violence takes place at or near the victim's home, as presented by the Bureau of Justice Statistics. Under the Violence Against Women Act, a landlord cannot evict a tenant who is the victim of domestic violence. It's important to check your local county and municipality for additional landlord-tenant regulations.

Unfortunately, that wasn't the end of it. After I didn't respond to his phone calls, my boyfriend found me again and this time took me by force from my apartment and brought me to his place. I knew if he got me alone at his place, he would severely hurt or even kill me.

As we approached his apartment, there were other residents outside. As I passed them, I started to scream and asked them to please help me and call the police. They tried to grab me away from him, but his strength won out and he dragged me by my feet into his apartment. I was so afraid I was going to die. The look on his face—I remember it as if it just happened yesterday. He was standing in the corner of the living room walking back and forth, telling me it was all my fault.

After a few moments of being in the apartment, I heard the neighbors outside saying they were calling the police as I stood by the window. It became deadly silent in the house. We locked eyes with each other and all I was thinking about was how to get out. I cannot explain what happened next but there was some kind of a force by me. Was it my guardian angel? I had no doubt in my mind that I was going to be hurt or even killed. Somehow, I went through the window. I can't remember how. You can say it was the adrenaline, but Someone got me out of that window with only a few scratches to my hand and cheek. I believe in higher powers, whether you call them angels or spirit guides. The police, of course, saw to it that I got home safely, and arrested my abuser.

It would be nice if that was the end of my relationship with him, but it wasn't. He was soon released from custody, although he didn't try to contact me. Shortly after starting my new job, I learned I was pregnant with his child.

I was in a big mess. I was single and pregnant, carrying the child of the man who abused me. Sooner or later I knew I would have to tell him. Legally, he had a right to know. At least I could wait for an advantageous time to contact him.

Truthfully, a part of me was happy that I was going to have a child. Finally, I would have someone I could love who would love me back.

Eventually, I told him. Foolishly, I allowed him back into my life. I didn't allow him into my apartment, but I traveled back and forth between his home and mine. I kept my new address and job secret for quite a while. Fortunately, while I was pregnant, his outbursts were manageable . . . for a while. I felt so alone and scared through the pregnancy. I didn't know what to expect, as I had no mother to call. I pretty much had to rely on books to get me through. The only person in my life whom I could turn to for support was—believe it or not—the man who had abused me! My girlfriend who had helped me find a new job and apartment was one of my angels, but I couldn't reach out. She was planning a wedding at the time, and I was so happy for her. I couldn't cause her any distress.

I had to get through it somehow. I was so stressed out not knowing what to do and how to get out of it while pregnant. In retrospect, I wish I'd had the courage to ask my brothers to help me. But part of me felt ashamed for getting myself into this mess. I felt that both my unborn child and I were trapped.

Soon after, while working on my property one afternoon, I went into labor. I called the father, who rushed me to the hospital. He seemed so happy that the baby was coming and made sure I was in good care.

I started my labor not knowing what to expect. The pain was so intense and scary. The doctor came in and asked me if I wanted something for the pain. I said "Yes!"

At that moment, the father spoke up and said, "No, she won't have any pain meds—she'll go through this naturally."

"That is not your decision," the doctor told him. Then the doctor turned to me and asked me again. Of course, I said yes, I wanted the medication. When the doctor left, my abusive boyfriend told me he wanted me to feel all the pain that I had put him through. I was stupefied; I was the one in labor, yet he was trying to make it all about him!

At that very moment, some special friends walked into the room. I had met the older couple through church, and they had become my mentors. They knew the history with my boyfriend's abuse. I have no idea how they found out I was in labor, but I was so happy to see them. They were my angels at that right moment. They must have seen the fear on my face, because the wife stayed with me while the husband took the baby's father out of the room. I started to cry so hard and told her what had happened. She looked at me and said she would not leave my side and if I wanted an epidural for the pain there was nothing wrong with it. Many mothers have this procedure during labor. She called in the doctor, and they started the process to get me the pain medication. While this was going on, the father returned to the room and caused a scene. The doctor called security and they escorted him out of the room. I was so relieved.

After twelve hard hours of labor, I had my baby: a beautiful baby girl I named Alyssa. I cried so hard. I could not believe how beautiful and precious she was. I was ready to take care of her even if I had to do it alone. God brought my church family to the hospital at the right time so this little beautiful angel could be born without any distractions. God had a plan for her life, to touch people for His purpose.

After leaving the hospital, I returned home and to my job as a property manager. I managed to take off two weeks to be home with my baby. I had a very limited income so I could only take a little time off work. I was so happy but also so scared. Sadly, none of my family came to visit us. I had told one of my brothers early in my pregnancy when I had the chance. I had to make that call when I was away from the house. I had even called my adoptive father and brother from the hospital after I had the baby. I was able to call because the baby's father had been escorted out and wasn't allowed back in the room. I had my church family there to help me make the calls. My adoptive father did not seem that excited for me when I spoke to him, but I was OK with that. It was just my baby girl and me. We were going to make it one way or another. At least, my birth mother served as a role model for what not to do. Unlike Helen, I was going to break the cycle of abandonment.

Of course, my abusive boyfriend was once again part of my—our—lives. Over the next few months, the father of my child managed to help me, and things were very peaceful. But that didn't last for long. His abusive, controlling ways were starting to resurface. I could sense his temper building again. One evening, I did not cook the right dinner for him, and he complained that I was not giving him enough attention. During the evening, his anger started to build when I didn't give into him. He grabbed me by my throat and started to choke me, holding me up against the wall. I felt certain that this time I was going to die! All I could think about was how my precious little girl, who was in the next room sleeping, would grow up without me.

After his anger had passed, I realized that I had to get us out. It was not about me staying in an abusive relationship—now there was an innocent child I had to make the right choices for, to keep her safe. I made a plan over the next week. I knew I had to be extremely careful. As I mentioned, the most dangerous time for a victim of abuse is when she tries to leave. Even more importantly, I had to protect my daughter, which made everything even more fraught!

On Wednesday evenings we always went to church, but during the day I faked being very ill and he agreed that I could stay home with the baby. I had a good friend who also attended the church and was aware of my situation. She had encouraged me to get out and was willing to help.

As we'd planned, my friend called me and informed me that my boyfriend had arrived at church. I knew it took forty-five minutes each way to drive to and from church, so I had to pack only what I needed. Although it was my apartment, I knew we wouldn't be safe there. I immediately started packing only essential things—clothes for me and documents that included our birth certificates and Social Security cards. Then I packed baby clothes, diapers, baby food, and a few toys. My car was very unreliable, but I had no choice. I would call my boss the next day and resign; I could not come back. I had to leave all my other possessions behind. I put my baby and myself in the packed car and prayed it would start. There was no Plan B if the car wouldn't work. After a few attempts, it started.

I drove to the next town and called the police and said I needed to find a safe place to stay. I explained what was going on. I was given the phone number and address of a shelter in Denver. I had to call them first to see if they had space for us. They had space and instructed me to park my car in the back of the building when I arrived. Since I was familiar with Denver, I knew I would find it. My daughter and I arrived at the shelter at about 9:00 p.m. that evening.

I felt so alone, but I knew my baby and I were in a safe place at last. I felt so horrible having to quit my job with no notice, especially because my boss had been good to me, but I had to do it to protect us. I soon learned that my ex took the furniture left in my apartment and sold many of my items, pocketing the money. The remainder he gave away to his relatives. But it didn't matter to me if my child was safe!

Sometimes I look back at how many times I had to abandon my belongings. I've had to replace expensive items like sofas and kitchen tables multiple times. No wonder I've had to struggle with money so often!

My daughter and I stayed in the shelter for about two months. The staff helped me to get a PFA (Protection from Abuse) order. I had to go to court with my daughter and face her father. But, supported by the staff of the shelter, I felt strong and determined for the first time. My ex tried to find us by going to my adoptive mother's house with a gun, but we were not there, thank goodness. He put my brothers in danger; it was my little brother who got the gun away from my ex. The strength my brother had that day is something I will never forget. I kept in touch by phone with my pastor, and he put me in touch with a very special family who took my daughter and me into their home. Another pair of angels, Sheila and Dave—I will always love them both! We stayed with them for about a year. I had to go back and forth to court so many times to fight for custody of my daughter. My ex was fighting for it only to control me. It was stressful, but the court fight for my daughter was worth every second to make sure she would be in a good, safe environment.

After a long time, I was finally granted custody. However, they awarded him visitation rights every other weekend. We would meet at the church for the drop-off, and for about a month, it went well. Then I received a call at work from my daughter's day care that they had concerns about nightmares she'd started to have during nap time. She was around two years old at the time. That day I quickly obtained an attorney, and he was able to get the visitations stopped until we went to court. I did not let my daughter go to my abuser's house again, but I had to be very careful because I knew he would be upset, especially once he was served with legal papers. Because of the history between us, with the police calls and the Protection from Abuse court orders, and the fact that I was a credible witness, the courts ordered supervised visitations for my daughter and her father to be held only through the children's hospital at his expense. This went on for about three months. Then he said he couldn't afford to pay anymore and all visits stopped. But that wasn't the end of his abuse. He phoned me frequently, and his calls grew increasingly serious and concerning.

I decided that I had to come up with a plan to leave. The company I had worked for had other locations out of state, and I asked for a transfer to Florida, even though I had to pay for all my moving expenses. As it happened, one of our residents was traveling to Florida to become a police officer! He said we could follow him, as his family lived very close to where we were going. Another angel.

The night before, I packed the car and hid it in one of the garages where I lived. I did not sleep well that night, worried my ex would be waiting somewhere on the property in the early hours and he wouldn't let us leave. I had to protect my baby! We left at four the next morning. It was a long, hard drive with an infant. My unreliable car broke down in Texas, but finally we made it, thanks to help from our angel.

We stayed in Florida for about eighteen months. I had to make a new life for us. My level of trust in other people was very low. For my daughter's sake, I had to be careful who entered our life. My contact with anyone outside of work was limited. Thankfully, our new life was very peaceful.

I put my daughter in a Christian day care only a few minutes from my job. I had to work but needed to ensure she was close to me so I could get her quickly if needed. I had to work very hard to help us get what we needed to survive. It was so different living in Florida. It was hot, and the Christmas we had in Florida was very different: our Christmas tree was a palm tree. Back in Colorado, tenants would complain of cockroaches and ask for an exterminator. In Florida, the cockroaches were even larger, especially the palmetto roaches, and they can fly. We all hated the cockroaches in Florida! But Florida also has more wildlife. Imagine a tenant calling you to remove an alligator! They can be found in any body of water. Where we lived had a lot of ponds on the property. I remember one day walking out of the house and one of the maintenance employees telling us to go back into the house because they had to capture a large snake. All in all, I have to say that I prefer the mountains of Colorado to the flatlands of Florida.

I was promoted to assistant manager while living in Florida, but soon after, the company I worked for lost the contract to manage that property. They had no other properties in Florida, so they gave me the option of returning to Denver. With hesitation, I agreed, as it would keep me employed. Back to Denver we went. I was able to get us our own apartment at a discount since I worked at the property, but I was always watching over my shoulder in fear that my ex would learn we were back.

One afternoon, after a couple months back in Denver, my daughter came running up to me and said, "Look, Mommy, my daddy is on TV!" My heart sank. He was on the news and under arrest for the murder of his own son—a child from a previous marriage. I quickly turned off the TV so my daughter wouldn't see it, and to this day it is a difficult subject to broach for anyone involved.

A few hours later, I received a phone call from a district attorney on the case wanting to meet with me to get some history on my ex and the abuse. How had they found me? I eventually received a summons to appear in court for the trial as a character witness. A character witness can testify on behalf of another as to that person's positive or negative character traits and the person's reputation in the community. This type of witness is often used in criminal cases.

The day of the trial, I was a nervous wreck as I was going to be face-to-face with my longtime abuser, and the only objective I had was protecting my daughter from him. Reporters and cameras swarmed all over the place, as he'd been accused of a horrific crime. My ex had a previous marriage with two children. There was a lot of abuse with this relationship as well, which I learned about after we had gotten together. In court, I was called up and had to stand in front of the judge and give a little history of the abuse that I had suffered with my ex, and all I had gone through to protect my child and keep her safe. My ex was sitting at a table to my right and had shackles placed round his ankles and hands. Even with those on him, I was terrified as I knew how strong he was. I made sure not to make eye contact with him.

His ex and her family were sitting in the courtroom. The hearing lasted a few weeks. At the sentencing hearing, my ex received eighty-three years in prison. The judge said he was a monster and he belonged behind bars. His ex and her family were able to have some kind of justice, but the pain of losing a family member will forever be with them no matter how long he will be in prison.

Finally my daughter and I could stay in one place, with no more running, no more hiding. No more abuse! We could have the semblance of a peaceful life. I would not have to look over my shoulder for the next eighty-three years.

From time to time, I still have a bad dream about him and the hurt he imposed on me. I will never forget it, but I have forgiven him so I can move on with my life. This part of my life was a bad storm that I did not want to go through. I now realize the only way I made it out alive was that God was holding my hand the entire time. He gave me the wisdom and strength to get out of the storm. Strength comes from overcoming events you can't imaging ever getting through. And I will not allow someone else's actions to harden my heart.

Chapter Thirteen

Helen and Me, Years Later

After my abuser went to prison, life smoothed out and became so much better for my daughter and me. Because of the vulnerability that had consumed me with my last relationship, however, I built walls around my heart, and I was fearful to enter another relationship.

So I went through counseling to help me heal through the trauma of all the abuse. I wanted to ensure I would never get involved in this type of relationship again. I believe with all my heart God brought my daughter to me at that exact moment to "wake me up," trusting me to make sure she would have a good life. Over time, my confidence started to build up again.

Unexpectedly I met a man who was much different than my last boyfriend. He was kind, and our values were the same. He was also hardworking like me. This relationship was different—there was love and respect between us. Still, it took a very long time before I would even let him meet my daughter. But over time, he became the dad to my daughter that she deserved. He spoiled her with so much love! It was very hard for me to believe that I could have a relationship that did not involve abuse. My walls were still up, and it took time for me to trust again, but we eventually got married and had a daughter together.

After a few years in Denver, my husband's employment closed their doors, and we had to make some hard decisions for our family. He had two job offers, one in New York and one in Pennsylvania. His family lived in Pennsylvania, so we choose this option. Family was important to us, and this would give my daughters the option to have a relationship with their dad's family. It was a very good choice, and we moved to Pennsylvania in 1996. Work options were a lot better for me, and doors opened in the corporate world. Life settled into a normal routine for the first time, although I still had some unanswered questions.

So I got in touch with my birth mother through the Denver Confidential Intermediary Program. In this program, the court can appoint someone to perform a search for birth parents. My appointed person found my birth mother and called me on July 4, 2003. I remember this day as if it just happened because I was in disbelief when I received the call. My family and I were heading out to see the fireworks as we always did every Fourth of July. My caseworker had located my mother by finding my birth cousin, the one I lived with for a short time, my aunt Rachel's youngest son. He gave the caseworker my mother's phone number, and she told me that my mother was shocked and really did not want to talk to me.

Also my caseworker learned there was another child, and my mother became very upset when my caseworker told her that it was the law that all siblings must be made aware of each other. If she did not honor the law, she would be taken to court. Finally, my mother had to face the consequences of her hateful, selfish choice of leaving her three children in foster care because she was pregnant and in a relationship. She had to tell her daughter about us and let us talk if we chose to.

All lies come out sooner or later.

Helen and I communicated by phone and email for some time. Finally, I made the trip from Pennsylvania to Colorado to see her. We scheduled our meeting for one morning at her home, where she lived alone. I remember that I changed into about six different outfits, wanting the perfect look. I was filled with so many emotions.

When I arrived, I was surprised at how nice her home was. I was expecting her to be living in the same sort of poverty I remembered from when I was a child, but her home did not look like it belonged to someone desperate enough to steal VA benefits from children. By an odd coincidence, she had the exact living room set that I had at my own home.

Helen received me cordially, and we sat and talked. I tried to ask her about what had happened in our past and why we couldn't be with her. All she told me was that she did not remember that time. Only later, after gaining access to my adoption records years later, did I find out why she said that. She gave up my brothers and me. She never showed up for the court hearing to get us back. She never told them about the VA monthly benefit payments she was getting from my father. Social Services could have found my father with that information. Helen's fourth child is eight years younger than I. She would have been born in 1969; I mentioned earlier that my mother was supposed to appear in court in early 1970, but she never showed. My stepsister was born, and this is why Helen did not come to court to get her three children back.

My mother knew the story, but she did not want to be honest with me about what she did when we had our first meeting together after all those years. She had the opportunity to tell me the truth during our visit and she blew it. I feel she did this because she didn't want to be called a liar or to make herself look bad in front of my stepsister. She clearly had no concern back then for her other three children. That obviously hadn't changed. But we kept our talk pleasant.

After we spoke, Helen suggested we meet with my stepsister, Cindy. I readily agreed. Of course, Cindy also had a complicated relationship as a child with Helen, but eventually they forged a good mother-daughter relationship. Helen had left Cindy's father, who soon after passed away.

I finally met my stepsister at her home. As with my mother, the meeting was very civil. As it approached lunchtime, the three of us went out to a restaurant. My mother seemed somewhat standoffish, but Cindy grew friendlier the longer we talked. The three of us parted on good terms.

Cindy stayed in touch and later spoke to my little brother. She seemed to genuinely want to establish a relationship with us. She and her husband even came out to Pennsylvania for Thanksgiving to meet my family. My stepsister and I cooked Thanksgiving dinner together; it brought joy to my heart to have this connection.

My two daughters were supportive but concerned. They knew the history between Helen and me. Most of all, they were afraid that Helen would hurt me again.

And then something went wrong.

I still can't say for sure what happened. After all, we lived more than two thousand miles apart. We rarely saw each other in person. I was the one who went to visit Helen on two trips. She never came to see me. She said in the past she was on planes so much and she didn't want to get on another one. As I look back, that statement should have told me that I was not worth the trip, but we spoke on the phone once a week.

My younger brother, Victor, was happy to build a relationship with Helen and Cindy. As mentioned earlier,

Victor has Legg-Calvé-Perthes disease and still has many challenges in his life. I'm very protective of him. Perhaps the break between Helen and I was over Victor. He had also visited Helen, and she made it very clear that she wanted no responsibility for someone with a disability.

I feel that Helen was behind the breakup between my stepsister and me. But less than two years after we all got in touch, we were no longer speaking to each other.

My stepsister used her dog as an excuse. She said that she was a dog lover and couldn't relate to anyone who wasn't. When I visited her house that first time, I told her I feared big dogs and could not be around her Rottweiler. I found this a strange thing to use as an excuse. Was she afraid that Helen and I would get too close? What a strange way to end what I thought was a good start to a relationship. I had opened my heart to her and so had my children. But I have to say, my girls advised me to be very careful as they did not want me to be hurt again.

Months later, I had to call Helen about some questions I had about health issues my brother was having. I wanted to get some family history. During the call, I opened up and asked Helen about Cindy and told her that she'd sent a disturbing get-well card to my brother. The card depicted a baby with a rattle, crying. I felt that the image and her comments on the card indicated that Cindy felt that Victor was not actually sick, and he should stop acting like a baby! Helen immediately grew argumentative, protecting

Cindy. In the heat of the argument, she blurted out how she really felt. She said, "You're fifty years old. Grow up. I'm not your mom! I'll never be your mom!"

Which just about says it all, doesn't it? I have not reached out to Helen since that day. I found her once; she did not look for me. I no longer believe that Helen and I will ever have a good relationship. She gave birth to me and my brothers but simply did not want anything to do with us—a heartbreaking realization for anyone to deal with, no matter how old.

It took some time, but I have finally forgiven my birth mother. Forgiveness is not for the other person; it's for you. It was time to let go of all the hurt and move on with my life, so that I could be the very best version of myself by showing love and kindness to all.

And the old wounds started to heal. I only wish her peace and happiness wherever she may be. We stumbled across each other's path for a reason, but God had a different path for me that I needed to take.

Now, by faith, I am an overcomer.

EPILOGUE

One Life

I have experienced a lot of darkness in my life. I have been through challenging situations, and sometimes I have hit bottom emotionally and spiritually. As I look back, I have had to transmute dark into light to get through it. For many years, I felt like I was caught up in a world in which I did not belong. I had to trust and believe in myself and trust that God was dealing with my enemies. When I look back and see where I am today, I know I've had to work extremely hard to forgive many people and still have love. It was not always easy to love. Many times, I thought there was something wrong with me.

Most of my guardians made bad choices. My birth mother, who felt that her life was more important than her two sons and her daughter, made the choice to abandon us. My aunt simply declined to care for us, and all these decisions led to us being relegated to Social Services. I have nothing but good things to say about my foster family, the Williamses. They came into our life at the right moment to help us through the rejection by showing us love and kindness. Then the state of Colorado made it impossible for us to stay with them. We were finally adopted, but my adoptive parents made bad choices as well. They were professional people who surely knew that I would benefit from a speech therapist and tutor, yet they never got me the help I needed. After they were divorced, I felt they had washed their hands of me.

When I dropped out of school and became an emancipated minor, I was the one who made decisions for myself. I also made some bad choices. My only excuse is that I rarely had good role models. If my marriage was fractious, so was the marriage of my birth parents. Ultimately, so was the marriage of my adoptive parents.

While I made some bad decisions, I did my best to correct those wrongs. I dropped out of school but eventually got my GED. I had a speech defect, but as a young adult, I worked hard to overcome it. A few words still trip me up, but most people who hear me speak today have no idea I had speech problems in my youth. And yet I felt stupid and embarrassed in school and made choices that reflected those feelings. I got married at such a young age it seemed doomed to fail.

But I learned from my mistakes and those of others. I learned that I could not give up on my own daughters. After my first child was born, I struggled a lot, having to work multiple jobs to survive with no college education—but not once did I think it would be easier for me to give up my child. I fought hard to protect my daughters. I have worked hard to try and be a good role model for them, to help guide them down the right pathway to be the very best they can be. Things were easier with my second daughter, as I was in a much better place. I stopped the bad choices of my birth family and didn't repeat the patterns I'd seen. I did everything I could to help my own daughters thrive. I believe I have succeeded when I look at the hardworking, kind, humble women they are today.

My second daughter was also the result of my working to make better decisions. In 1993, I married James and we have been married ever since. I am proud that my marriage has worked and the vows we took have lasted. We still have a strong love, and it makes me proud. We have built a good life together. That my husband took on the responsibility of helping to raise my firstborn tells you a lot about the man whom I married. I made a great choice! My husband and I had our second precious, beautiful daughter, Troylynn. I am so grateful! She has a beautiful, kind heart and loves to help children by teaching.

I was born Troy and my middle name was Lynn. I combined them as one name for my daughters. The name Troylynn is a very powerful word to me because I was born with that name. I was an unwanted child, but I broke the cycle of what my birth mother did. My firstborn is Alyssa Troylynn and my second daughter is Troylynn Mary. They are dearly loved and wanted with all my heart! Troylynn survived and lives through me and my beautiful daughters.

Message to My Readers

There are some of us who believe in a higher power and then there are some who disbelieve in the existence of God or gods. One of my family members is an atheist and that's OK with me; I still love them. It's not for me to judge those beliefs. For me, however, I will follow God. One day God is going to take me home and when I get there, I believe that I will finally understand why my one life had so many challenges. I had to go through the pain to help that one person, or maybe many, so I could feel exactly what they are feeling. I can relate to someone who has experienced the abandonment of a parent, or physical or mental abuse, or being on their own at an early age. The feeling of not being wanted at the beginning of your life sets the stage for so much rejection to come. My readers, we all go through our own challenges.

The only way I made it this far was to always push myself, be resilient, and to have perseverance. I never quit. No, it was not easy, but you only have one life and it's up to you to make it the best one possible! If I did it, so can you! You are all amazing! My happiness has always been to help people in need around me. There are people who are going through something worse than what I went through. Just a smile could mean the world to someone going through a hard time. I have always tried to choose my words carefully, as I do not know the road someone has gone down, and it might be my words that save a person's life. Kindness and love never go wrong!

Now, at last, I have a supportive, loving family. They are my proudest, greatest achievement. I am so very proud of them all!

All children are a gift from God. I will do my best to support them always.

As for me, the lesson learned after my abusive relationship is to keep kind people close to me. My passion is to help children going through adoption and women going through abuse. Now I can share my story, having lived through those same challenges. I went to night school to get my paralegal certificate in order to help them. For some time, I worked at a domestic violence center helping women and children to get PFAs (Protection from Abuse orders).

Today, I work for a company that is helping patients. I also sponsor a child and volunteer at shelters. I always work hard doing my best each day, being a team player, smiling, and being positive. Through hard work, I climbed the ladder to become a senior executive assistant supporting a wonderful team. I will always look for opportunities to help serve people. I always believe God will put me in the right situation at the right moment to help others. It has already happened many times. There are so many people in this world going through the same challenges; it's how we see each situation and how we react that is the key to our survival. As I said earlier, when God takes me back to Him, I truly believe it's going to be the people I helped on this earth who will be there to welcome me.

Throughout my life, people have asked me, "What planet are you from? How can you see such kindness in everything?" Maybe I am not from the same place as you, but I needed to be in a world that needed my kindness. I call myself a lightworker; they are simply everywhere with a deep calling to help people.

Trust me, I have had my moments! However, I tell myself there are others who have it worse. Through it all, I am so thankful that I still have a kind heart and want to help others. I truly believe we are not on this earth for ourselves. Rather, we are here to help those who need help. We all have a task each and every day of our one life, and mine is to help and serve others. Just look around—all of us can help others!

I have heard that near the end of life we have a flashback, like a slide show. It consists of good memories but also the mistakes we wish we could take back. I know that I've been wronged, but I choose not to hold on to anger. Instead, I forgive those who gave up on me at the beginning of my life. God has taken the broken pieces in me created by abandonment and assembled them into a mosaic masterpiece, turning the things meant for ill into a beautiful opportunity to help others. If I can change just one person's life and the challenges they are going through with this book, then my purpose has been fulfilled and it has all been worth it. I want to leave a legacy of love and kindness through helping people.

To My Family

Finally, a message to my daughters and grandbabies, from oldest to youngest:

Alyssa and Troylynn: When I tell you both that I love you, I don't say it out of habit or to make conversation. I say it to remind you both that you are the best thing that ever happened to me. I am so very proud of you both, for the beautiful, kind, hard-working women you have become. Don't ever change! Always be yourselves—the kind, loving people you are. I am so thankful that I was chosen to be your mom!

Alyssa, you have a laugh that is so contagious it makes everyone laugh. Always keep that laugh. You are such a beautiful mother, in some ways better than I ever was. As a nurse, everyone you help is truly blessed. Always look after your sister too! You're always in my heart, my special daughter! I am so grateful to be your mother!

Troylynn, your beautiful smile lights up for all to see. Don't ever lose that! You are an amazing writer and teacher, and have touched many lives! You are the best aunt my grandbabies could ever have, always making them feel special and spending quality time with them. You're always in my heart, my special daughter! I am so grateful to be your mother!

Josiah and Alana, grandchildren are a grandparent's link to the future, and grandparents are the child's link to the past.

Josiah, you're an amazing grandson with such a kind heart. Always be you because God has a perfect plan for your life to touch many people. Work hard at everything you set your mind to, and many doors will open. You're also an amazing track star; always have confidence in yourself. Also keep kind people around you. Thank you for all our adventures in keeping me young. I am so proud of you, and it is such a blessing to be your mum-mum. I love you so much!

Alana, you're such an amazing granddaughter, who has a kind heart. You have a smile that lights up a room when you enter. Work hard to reach your dreams. God also has the perfect plan for your life to touch many people. Always have confidence to know your self-worth. Learn everything you can. Keep kind people close to you. Thank you for keeping me young with all our adventures. I am so proud of you, and it is such a blessing to be your mum-mum. I love you so much!

One Life

We all come into this world with nothing but love.
We come at our exact moment with a purpose.
We all will have challenges throughout our life;
We have to choose our pathway, right or wrong.
We all will have triumphs and defeats;
We get to choose how to react to those challenges.
We get to choose forgiveness or unforgiveness for
those who have hurt us.
We get to choose how much love and kindness we give
out to others unselfishly
Before God says it's time to go home.

Elizabeth Troy Lynn

To the reader:

Thank you for reading my story. I am truly humbled.

I finally dare to share my story.

Some of the darkness that I went through did not destroy me, but it strengthened me to discover who I really am and my purpose on earth. I want to always help people through love and kindness. Some will be one step behind me, facing their own challenges. They need to know they are not alone.

Life is so short. Your life is your story to write. You hold power to stop and edit it at any time. I hope that sharing my story will encourage people never to give up, trust God, and always believing in themselves!

Thank you!
Elizabeth Troylynn

About the Author

Elizabeth TroyLynn was born and raised in the beautiful mountain state of Colorado. She is a wife, mother, and grandmother who loves the outdoors. She is a former paralegal and began writing in 2017. *His Mosaic Masterpiece*, her first book, depicts a life of abuse and abandonment overcome through determination and faith. Elizabeth's faith and family have been the utmost important aspects of how she turned from a victim into a victor. Elizabeth hopes that this book will be an inspiration to many around the world.